CW00662564

Hymns for the Poor of the Flock [Compiled by Sir E. Denny]

HYMNS

FOR

THE POOR OF THE FLOCK.

LONDON:

PRINTED BY JOHN WERTHEIMER AND CO.,
CIRCUS PLACE, FINSBURY CIRCUS.

HYMNS

FOR

THE POOR OF THE FLOCK.

———

" I will sing with the spirit, and I will sing with the
understanding also."—1 Cor. xiv. 15.

———

LONDON :

CENTRAL TRACT DEPOT,

1, WARWICK SQUARE,

1840.

197.

INDEX.

--- — ---

SPECIAL OCCASIONS.

BAPTISM.

CHRISTIAN SABBATH.

HYMNS.

I.—8, 7.

1 GLORY, glory everlasting,
   Be to Him Who bore the cross,
  Who redeem'd our souls by tasting
   Death, the death deserv'd by us!
     Spread His glory
   Who redeem'd His people thus.

2 His is love, 'tis love unbounded,
   Without measure, without end;
  Human thought is here confounded;
   'Tis too vast to comprehend:
     Praise the Saviour!
   Magnify the sinners' friend.

3 While we tell the wondrous story
   Of the Saviour's cross and shame,
  Sing we—" Everlasting glory
   Be to God and to the Lamb."
     Saints and angels,
   Give ye glory to His name.

II.—8s.

1 WE 'LL sing of the Shepherd that died,
  That died for the sake of the flock;
His love to the utmost was tried,
  But firmly endur'd as a rock.

2 When blood from a victim must flow
  This Shepherd, by pity, was led
To stand between us and the foe,
  And willingly died in our stead.

3 Our song then for ever shall be,
  Of the Shepherd who gave Himself thus;
No subject's so glorious as He,
  No theme 's so affecting to us.

4 We 'll sing of such subjects alone,
  None other our tongues shall employ;
Till better His love becomes known,
  In yonder bright regions of joy.

III.—7, 7, 8, 7. bis.

1 HEAD of the church triumphant!
  We joyfully adore Thee,
    'Till Thou appear
    Thy members here

Would sing like those in glory!
We lift our hearts and voices,
In blest anticipation,
   And cry aloud,
   And give to God
The praise of our salvation.

2 While in affliction's furnace
  And passing through the fire;
    The love we praise
    Which tries our ways,
  And ever brings us nigher;
  We clap our hands, exulting
. In Thine almighty favour:
    The love divine
    Which makes us Thine,
  Shall keep us Thine for ever.

3 Thou dost conduct Thy people,
  Through torrents of temptation;
    Nor will we fear,
    While Thou art near,
  The fire of tribulation:
  The World, with Sin and Satan,
  In vain our march opposes;
    By Thee we shall
    Break through them all,
  And sing the song of Moses.

4 By faith we see the glory
  Of which Thou dost assure us,
    The world despise
    For that high prize
  Which Thou hast set before us;
  And if Thou count us worthy,
  We each would die like Stephen,
    And see Thee stand
    At God's right hand,
  To take us up to heaven.

IV.—8, 7.

1 Lo! He comes, with clouds descending.
  Once for favor'd sinners slain!
Thousand thousand saints attending,
  Swell the triumph of His train!
    Hallelujah!
  Jesus comes and comes to reign!

2 Now redemption, long expected,
  See in solemn pomp appear!
All His saints, by man rejected,
  Rise to meet Him in the air.
    Hallelujah!
  See the day of God appear!

3 Israel, too, shall now behold Him,
    Full of grace and majesty,
Tho' they set at nought and sold Him,
    Pierc'd and nail'd Him to the tree,
      Now returning,
    He their lov'd Messiah 'll be.

4 Answer Thine own Bride and Spirit,
    Hasten, Lord, and quickly come;
The glory promis'd to inherit,
    Take Thy waiting people home.
      All creation
    Travails, groans, and bids Thee come.

5 Yea, Amen, let all adore Thee,
    High on Thine exalted throne:
Saviour, take the power and glory:
    Claim the kingdoms for Thine own:
      O come quickly!
    Hallelujah! come, Lord, come!

V.—6, 6, 4.
6, 6, 6, 4.

1 GLORY to God on High!
  Let Heav'n and Earth reply,
    " Praise ye His name !"

5

All Heaven's hosts adore
Him Who our sorrows bore,
Crying for evermore,
" Worthy the Lamb !"

2 They who surround the throne
Blissfully join in one,
Praising His name.
We too, who know His blood
Hath sealed our peace with God,
Will sound His fame abroad,
" Worthy the Lamb !"

3 Join, all the ransom'd race,
Our Lord and God to bless,
" Praise ye His name !"
Tell what His arm hath done!
What spoils from death He won!
Sing His great name alone!
" Worthy the Lamb !"

4 Jesus, our Lord and God,
Bore sin's tremendous load,
" Praise ye His name !"
In Him will we rejoice,
Making a cheerful noise,
And shout with heart and voice,
" Worthy the Lamb !"

5 And if we change our place,
   Yet shall we never cease
     Praising His name;
   But still the offering
   Of praise to Him shall bring,
   And without ceasing sing
     " Worthy the Lamb !"

VI.—7, 6.

O JESUS Christ, most holy—
   Head of the Church, Thy bride,
In us each day more fully
   Thy name be magnified !
O may, in each believer,
   Thy love its pow'r display,
And none amongst us ever
   From Thee, our Shepherd, stray !

VII.—8, 7.

1 " ABBA," Father,—Lord ! we call Thee,
   (Hallow'd name !) from day to day;—
'Tis Thy children's right to know Thee,
   None but children, "Abba," say.
This high glory we inherit,
   Thy free gift, through Jesus' blood;
God the Spirit, with our spirit,
   Witnesseth we 're Sons of God

2 Abba's purpose gave us being,
    When in Christ, in that vast plan,
Abba chose the church in Jesus,
    Long before the world began;
O what love the Father bore us!
    O how precious in His sight!—
When He gave His church to Jesus!
    Jesus, His whole soul's delight!

3 Though our nature's fall in Adam,
    Seem'd to shut us out from God,
Thus it was His counsel brought us
    Nearer still, thro' Jesus' blood;
For in Him we found redemption,
    Grace and Glory in the Son,
O the height and depth of Mercy!
    " Christ and the elect are one."

VIII.—SECOND PART.

1 RICHEST stores of Heav'nly blessings
    God has giv'n in Christ, His Son—
With the Holy Spirit's power,
    Safe to lead His children on.
"Abba," Father, makes all certain,
    E'en by word, and oath, and blood;—
Abba saith, " They *are* My children,"
    And they say, "Our Abba's GOD."

2 Hence, through all the changing seasons,
    Trouble, sorrow, sickness, woe,
Nothing changeth God's affection,
    Abba's love shall bring us through.
Soon shall all the blood-bought children,
    Round the throne their anthems raise ;
And, in songs of rich salvation,
    Shout to Abba endless praise.

CHORUS.

"Abba," Father! Lord, we'll call Thee,
    Abba 'll sound through all the host;
All in heav'n and earth adoring,
    Father, Son, and Holy Ghost!

IX.—7, 6.

1 ERE God had built the mountains,
    Or rais'd the fruitful hills,
Before He fill'd the fountains,
    That feed the running rills;
In Thee, from everlasting,
    The wonderful I AM
Found pleasures never wasting,
    And Wisdom is Thy name.

3 Jesus is worthy to receive
    Honour and pow'r divine:
And blessings more than we can give,
    Be, Lord, for ever Thine.

4 Let all that dwell above the sky,
    A joyful anthem raise,
Join to exalt Thy glories high,
    And speak Thine endless praise.

5 Redeem'd creation join in one,
    To bless the sacred name
Of Him that sits upon the throne,
    And to adore the Lamb.

XI.—10, 10, 11, 11.

1 THOUGH troubles assail,
    And dangers affright,
Though friends should all fail,
    And foes all unite:
Yet one thing secures us
    Whatever betide,
The Scripture assures us,
    The LORD will provide.

2 The birds without barn,
   Or storehouse are fed,
 ·From them let us learn
   To trust for our bread:
His saints, what is fitting,
   Shall ne'er be denied,
So long as 'tis written
   The LORD will provide.

3 We may, like the ships,
   By tempests be tost
On perilous deeps,
   But cannot be lost:
Though Satan enrages
   The wind and the tide,
The promise engages
   The LORD will provide.

4 His call we obey,
   Like Abram of old,
Not knowing our way,
   But faith makes us bold;
For though we are strangers,
   We have a sure guide,
And trust in all dangers
   The LORD will provide.

XII.—SECOND PART.

1 WHEN Satan appears
    To stop up our path,
  And fill us with fears,
    We triumph by faith;
  He cannot take from us,
    Though oft he has tried,
  This heart-cheering promise,—
    The LORD will provide.

2 He tells us we're weak,
    Our hope is in vain,
  The good that we seek
    We ne'er shall obtain;
  But when such suggestions
    Our spirits have tried,
  This answers all questions,—
    The LORD will provide.

3 No strength of our own
    Or goodness we claim;
  Yet since we have known
    The Saviour's great name,

In this our strong tower
  For safety we hide,
The LORD is our power,
  The LORD will provide.

4 Should life sink apace,
  And death be in view,
This word of his grace
  Shall comfort us through:
No fearing or doubting,—
  With CHRIST on their side
Who cannot die shouting,
  The LORD will provide?

XIII.—8, 7.

1 ONE there is, above all others,
  Well deserves the name of Friend!
His is love beyond a brother's,
  Costly, free, and knows no end:
They who once his kindness prove,
Find it everlasting love!

2 Which of all our friends to save us,
  Could or would have shed his blood?
But our Jesus died to have us
  Reconcil'd in Him to God:
This was boundless love indeed!
Jesus is a Friend in need.

3 When He liv'd on earth abased,
  "Friend of Sinners" was His name;
Now above all glory raised,
  He rejoices in the same:
Saints He calls His " brethren, friends,"
And to all their wants attends.

4 O! for grace our hearts to soften;
  Teach us, Saviour, love for love;
We, alas! forget too often,
  What a Friend we have above:
Thus may all Thy saints be taught,
How to love Thee as they ought.

XIV.—8, 8, 6. bis.

1 We bless Thee, O Thou great Amen!
Jehovah's pledge to sinful men,
  Confirming all His word!
Doubtful no promises remain,
For all are Yea, and all Amen,
  In Thee, our faithful Lord.

2 How great the grace of God to bless
By Thee, the Lord our righteousness!
  By Thee, we say again:
For to us all things thus are sure,
Through life, in death, and evermore,
  By Thee, the Great Amen.

3 O faithful Witness of our God,
  Who cam'st by water and by blood!
    In Thee (the Holy One)
  God's record doth for ever stand,
  Of life eternal, from His hand,
    To all in Thee the Son.

4 Gladly His promises we hear,
  For God's "Amen" dispels all fear,
    His faithfulness it proves;
  And while such grace from God is shown,
  To His Amen, we add our own:
    For our Amen He loves.

XV.—SECOND PART.

1 CHILDREN of God, in age or youth,
  Who live by Christ, the God of truth—
    Secure in Him remain;
  Make Him what He is made to you,
  Your Alpha and Omega too,
    God's Christ is your Amen.

2 Nor less above, ye heav'nly host!
  To Father, Son and Holy Ghost,
    Give praise for ransom'd men;
  For now to you, by them's made known,
  The richest wisdom ever shown,
    Thro' Christ, the Great Amen.

Secur'd in Him, the Church on High,
And saints below, may boldly cry,
  Praise to our God Amen!
To God in Christ all praise be giv'n—
For evermore on earth, in heav'n,
  Amen! Amen! Amen!

XVI.—7s.

1 BRETHREN, let us join to bless
  Jesus Christ, our joy and peace!
  Let our praise to Him be giv'n,
  High at God's right hand in heav'n.

2 Master, lo! to Thee we bow,
  Thou art Lord, and only Thou:
  Thou the virgin's blessed seed,
  Thou the Church's glorious Head.

3 Thee the angels ceaseless sing,
  Thee we praise, The Priest and King;
  Worthy is Thy name of praise,
  Full of glory, full of Grace!

4 Joyful tidings Thou hast brought,
  Of salvation, by Thee wrought:
  Wrought for all Thy church! and we
  Worship in their company.

c

5 We, Thy little flock, adore
 Thee, the Lord, for evermore!
 Ever resting in Thy love,
 'Till we join with those above.

XVII.—8, 7.

1 SAVIOUR, come, Thy Saints are waiting,
 Waiting for the nuptial day,
 Thence their promis'd glory dating;
 Come, and bear Thy saints away.
 Come, Lord Jesus,
 Thus Thy waiting people pray.

2 Base the wish, and vain th' endeavour,
 While on earth to find our rest;
 Till we see Thy face, we never
 Shall or can be fully blest;
 In Thy presence
 Nothing shall our peace molest.

3 Lord, we wait for thine appearing;
 "Tarry not" Thy people say;
 Bright the prospect is, and cheering,
 Of beholding Thee that day;
 When our sorrow
 Shall for ever pass away.

4 Till it comes, O keep us steady,
　　Keep us walking in Thy ways;
At Thy call may we be ready,
　　And our Heads with triumph raise;
　　　Then with angels
　　Sing Thine everlasting praise.

XVIII.—8s.

How good is the God we adore,
Our faithful unchangeable Friend,
Whose love is as great as His power,
And knows neither measure nor end!

'Tis Jesus, the First and the Last,
Whose Spirit shall guide us safe home;
We'll praise Him for all that is past,
And trust Him for all that 's to come.

XIX.—8, 7.

1 HAIL, Thou once-despised Jesus!
　　Hail, Thou Galilean king!
Thou didst suffer to release us;
　　Thou didst free salvation bring;
Thro' Thy death and resurrection,
　　Bearer of our sin and shame!
We enjoy Divine protection,
　　Life and glory through Thy name.

2 Paschal Lamb, by God appointed,
   All our sins on Thee were laid:
By Almighty Love anointed,
   Thou hast full atonement made:
We who trust Thee are forgiven,
   Through the virtue of Thy blood;
Rent in Thee the veil of heaven;
   Grace shines forth to man from God.

XX.—SECOND PART.

3 JESUS, hail! amid the glory,
   Where for us Thou dost abide;
(All the heav'nly hosts adore Thee!)
   Standing at Thy Father's side,
There for us Thou now art pleading;
   While Thou dost our place prepare,
For the church still interceding,
   Till in glory it appear.

4 Worship, honour, power, and blessing,
   Thou shalt then from all receive ;
Loudest praises, without ceasing,
   All that earth or heav'n can give:
'Till that day,—th' angelic spirits,
   With the church, in feebler lays,
Still shall try to sing Thy merits,
   And to chant Thy Father's praise.

XXI.—8s.

1 Now in a song of grateful praise,
   To our dear Lord the voice we 'll raise;
   With all His saints we 'll join to tell,
      " Our Jesus hath done all things well."

2 All worlds His glorious power confess,
   His wisdom all His works express ;
   But, O His love !—what tongue can tell ?
      " Our Jesus hath done all things well."

3 And since our souls have known His love,
   What mercies hath He made us prove,
   Mercies which all our praise excel;
      "Our Jesus hath done all things well."

4 Tho' many fiery flaming darts
   The tempter levels at our hearts,
   With this we all his rage repel,
      " Our Jesus hath done all things well."

5 And when on that bright day we rise,
   And join the anthems of the skies,
   Among the rest this note shall swell,
      " Our Jesus hath done all things well."

XXII.—8, 7.

1 NOTHING know we of the season,
　　When the world shall pass away;
But we know the saints have reason,
　　To expect a glorious day;
When the Saviour shall return,
And His people cease to mourn.

2 While a careless world is sleeping—
　　Then it is the Lord will come;
While His Saints the watch are keeping,
　　That they may escape its doom—
As admonish'd by the Word
Of their faithful loving Lord.

3 O what sacred joys await them!
　　They shall see the Saviour then;
Those who now oppose and hate them,
　　Never shall oppose again!
Brethren, let us think of this,
All is ours since we are His.

4 Being of the favour'd number
　　Whom the Saviour calls His own,
'Tis not meet that we should slumber,
　　Nothing should be left undone:
This should be His people's aim;
Still to glorify His name.

5 Waiting then, our Lord's returning,
    Be it ours His word to keep;
  Let our lamps be always burning,
    Let us watch while others sleep,
  We 're no longer of the night,
  We are children of the light.

XXIII.—8s.

1 'TWIXT Jesus and the chosen race
  Subsists a bond of sov'reign grace,
  A bond which hell's tremendous train,
  Can ne'er dissolve, or rend in twain.

2 This sacred bond shall never break,
  Though earth should to her centre shake;
  We rest in hope, assur'd of this,—
  For God has pledg'd His faithfulness.

3 He spake and sware;— and it was done,
  Wrought in the blood of His dear Son;
  The Lamb appointed to redeem
  All that the Father lov'd in Him.

4 O sacred union, firm and strong!
  How great the grace! how sweet the song
  That Adam's sons should ever be
  One with Incarnate Deity!

5 One in His death, one when He rose,
  One when He triumph'd o'er His foes,
  One when in heav'n He took His seat,
  And plainly prov'd all hell's defeat.

6 Triumphant thus o'er all its pow'rs,
  (For all He is and has is ours),
  With Him, our Head, we stand or fall,
  Our life, our surety and our all.

7 Thus sav'd in Him, a chosen race
  O may we prove our faithfulness—
  And live to Him in Whom we died,
  With Whom we shall be glorified.

XXIV.—8s.

1 On CHRIST, salvation rests secure;
  This Rock of Ages must endure;
  Nor can that faith be overthrown,
  Which rests upon the "Living Stone."

2 No other hope shall intervene:
  To Him we look, on Him we lean:
  Other foundations we disown,
  And build on Christ, the " Living Stone.

3 In Him, it is ordain'd to raise
  A temple to Jehovah's praise,

Compos'd of all the saints, who own
No Saviour but the " Living Stone."

4 View the vast building, see it rise;
The work how great! the plan how wise!
O wondrous fabric! pow'r unknown!
That rears it on the " Living Stone."

5 But most adore His precious name;
His glory and His grace proclaim :
For us, condemn'd, despis'd, undone,
He gave Himself, the " Living Stone."

XXV.—7, 7, 7, 5. bis.

1 MUCH in sorrow, oft in woe,
Onward, Christians, onward go;
Fight the fight! tho' worn with strife,
Battle on to life.
Onward, Christians! onward go;
Join the war, and face the foe;
Faint not, little doth remain
Of the drear campaign.

2 Shrink not, Christians : will you yield?
Will you quit the battle field?
Shrink not, ere the fight be done,
Ere the prize be won.

Mail'd in armour, heav'nly bright,
Strong in Him, Whose grace is might,
Onward, Christians, onward go,
    Conquer ev'ry foe.

3 Fight the glorious fight of faith,
Fear not conflict, fear not death ;
Conflict !—that but nerves to strife :
    Death !—to endless life !
Onward, Christians, onward go,
Scorning danger, shame, and woe;
Tread the path which they have trod
    Whose rest is now with God.

CHORUS.—6, 8.

We 're bound for the kingdom :
Let us hasten on to glory,
    And sing Hallelujah,
    Sing glory, hallelujah !

We're bound for the kingdom :
Let us onward press to glory,
    And sing Hallelujah
    To God and the Lamb !

XXVI.—8, 7.

1 GRACIOUS LORD, my heart is fixed;
  Sing I will, and sing of Thee,

27

Since the cup that justice mixed,
   Thou hast drank, and drank for me.
     Great Deliv'rer!
   Thou hast set the pris'ner free.

2 Many were the chains that bound me,
   But the Lord has loos'd them all :
Arms of mercy now surround me,
   Favours these, nor few nor small:
     Saviour, keep me!
   Keep Thy servant, lest he fall.

3 Fair the scene that lies before me ;
   Life eternal Jesus gives ;
While He waves His banner o'er me,
   Peace and joy my soul receives :
     Sure His promise!
   I shall live because He lives.

4 When the world would bid me leave Thee,
   Telling me of shame and loss,
Saviour, guard me lest I grieve Thee,
   Lest I cease to love Thy cross :
     This is treasure;
   All the rest I count but dross.

XXVII.—8s.

1 BLEST Lamb of God! with grateful praise
   Our voices now to Thee we raise—

On Earth to reign, redeem'd by Blood,
We, kings and priests, *are made* to God.—

2 Soon too, in glory shall we sing,
And louder praises to Thee bring—
While every nation, tongue and tribe,
Strength, glory, might,to Thee ascribe !
Amen! Amen!
Saviour! Amen!

XXVIII. 8s.

1 THE Saviour lives, no more to die;
He lives our Head, enthron'd on high ;
He lives triumphant o'er the grave ;
He lives eternally to save.

2 He lives to still His people's fears ;
He lives to wipe away their tears ;
He lives their mansions to prepare ;
He lives to bring them safely there.

3 Then let our souls in Him rejoice,
And sing His praise with cheerful voice:
Our doubts and fears for ever gone,
For Christ is on the Father's throne.

4 The chief of sinners He receives :
His saints He loves, and never leaves ;

He'll guard us safe from ev'ry ill,
And all His promises fulfil.

5 Abundant grace will He afford,
 Till we are present with the Lord,
 And prove what we have sung before,
 That Jesus lives for evermore.

XXIX.—8, 7.

1 PRAISE the Lord Who died to save us;
  Praise His name, for ever dear;
 'Twas by Him the Father gave us
  Eyes to see, and ears to hear:
   Praise the Saviour,
  Object of our love and fear.

2 Grace it was, 'twas Grace abounding,
  Brought Him down to save the lost;
 Ye above, the throne surrounding,
  Praise Him, praise Him all His host:
   Saints adore Him;
  Ye are they who owe Him most.

3 Ye, of all His hand created,
  Objects are of Grace alone;
 Aliens once, but reinstated;

Destin'd now to share His throne:
Sing with wonder;
Sing of what the Lord hath done.

4 Praise His name, Who died to save us;
'Tis by Him alone we live;
And in Him the Father gave us
All that boundless love could give :
Life eternal
In our Saviour we receive.

XXX.—6, 6, 6, 6, 8, 8.

1 Th' ATONING work is done;
The victim's blood is shed;
And Jesus now is gone
His people's cause to plead:
He stands in heav'n their great High Priest,
And bears their names upon His breast.

2 He sprinkled with His blood
The mercy-seat above;
For Justice had withstood
The purposes of Love;
But Justice now withstands no more,
And Mercy yields her boundless store.

3 No temple made with hands
His place of service is ;

In heav'n itself He stands,
A heav'nly priesthood His ;
In Him the shadows of the law
Are all fulfill'd, and now withdraw.

4 And though awhile He be
Hid from the eyes of men,
His people look to see
Their great High Priest again.
In brightest glory He will come,
And take His waiting people home.

XXXI.—8s.

1 *Let sinners sav'd give thanks and sing,*
Of mercies past, of joys to come ;
The Lord their Saviour is, and King,
The cross their stay, and heav'n their home.

2 *Let sinners sav'd give thanks and sing,*
Salvation 's theirs, and of the Lord ;
They draw from heav'n's eternal spring,
The living God, their great reward.

3 *Let sinners sav'd give thanks and sing ;*
Sweet is the subject of their song,
Who, made the children of a King,
Expect to sing in Heav'n ere long.

3 *Let sinners sav'd give thanks and sing,*
   Whom grace has kept in dangers past ;
   And, O sweet thought ! the Lord will bring
   His people safe to heav'n at last.

4 *Let sinners sav'd give thanks and sing,*
   Of Jesus sing, through all their days ;
   In heav'n their golden harps they 'll string,
   And there for ever sing His praise.

XXXII.—8s.

1 GREAT Shepherd of the chosen few,
   Thy former mercies here renew:
   And to our waiting hearts proclaim
   The sweetness of Thy saving name.

2 Now may we prove the power of prayer,
   To strengthen faith and banish care;
   To teach our faint desire to rise,
   And bring all heav'n before our eyes.

XXXIII.—6, 6, 8, 6.

1 AWAKE, and sing the song
   Of Moses and the Lamb:
   Wake ev'ry heart, and ev'ry tongue,
   To praise the Saviour's name.

2 Sing of His dying love ;
　　Sing of His rising pow'r ;
　Sing how He intercedes above,
　　For those whose sins He bore.

3 Sing on your heav'nly road,
　　Ye sons of Glory, sing ;
　To God and to the Lamb of God
　　Your cheerful praises bring.

4 Soon shall we hear Him say,
　　" Come, blessed brethren, come :"
　Soon will He call us hence away,
　　And take us to His home.

5 Then shall each raptur'd tongue
　　His fullest praise proclaim,
　And sweeter voices tune the song
　　Of Moses and the Lamb.

XXXIV.—8, 6.

1 BLESS'D be the everlasting God,
　　The Father of our Lord :
　Let His abounding grace be prais'd !
　　His majesty ador'd ! ·

D

2 When from the dead He rais'd His Son,
    And took Him to the skies,
He gave the Church a lively type
    How she at length should rise.

3 A type which bids us hope His grace
    Will raise us from the dust ;
And, ah ! sweet thought ! *as* Christ arose,
    So we His members must.

4 For tho' we know—all shall not die,
    Yet all a change must see ;
Since when we see Him as He is,
    Then shall we like Him be.

5 Nor death, nor life, nor earth, nor hell,
    Nor things that pass away,
Can ever change this finish'd type,
    Or make this hope decay.

6 The hope that we ere long shall share
    Christ's glory and His home,
Doth on the word of God depend
    Till the salvation come.

XXXV.—6, 6, 8, 6.

THE LORD IS RIS'N INDEED :
  Then Justice asks no more ;
Mercy and Truth are now agreed,
  Who stood oppos'd before.

THE LORD IS RIS'N INDEED :
  Then all His work's perform'd ;
The captive Surety now is freed,
  And Death, our foe, disarm'd.

THE LORD IS RIS'N INDEED :
  He lives—to die no more ;
He lives—His people's cause to plead,
  Whose curse and shame He bore.

THE LORD IS RIS'N INDEED :
  And Hell has lost its prey ;
And with Him all the ransom'd seed,
  Shall reign in endless day.

XXXVI.—8, 6.

1 BEHOLD the Lamb, with glory crown'd!
  To Him all pow'r is giv'n:
No place too high for Him is found,
  No place too high in heav'n.

2 With faces veil'd, the Seraphs bright,
  Did on His glory gaze;
Not Seraphs could endure the light,
  Of the resplendent blaze.

3 Well may His people then be found
  Transported with the sight;
To see their Lord with glory crown'd,
  Must yield them sweet delight.

4 Though high, yet He accepts the praise
  His people offer here:
The faintest, feeblest cry they raise,
  Will reach the Saviour's ear.

5 This song be ours, and this alone,
  That celebrates the name
Of Him that sits upon the throne
  And that exalts the Lamb.

6 To Him Whom men despise and slight,
  To Him be glory given:
The crown is His, and His by right
  The highest place in heaven.

XXXVII.—8, 7.

1 GUIDE us, O Thou great Jehovah!
  Pilgrims through this barren land;
We are weak, but Thou art mighty;
  Hold us by Thy pow'rful hand.
    Bread of heaven!
Feed us now and evermore.

2 Open stand, Thou living Fountain!
  Whence the healing waters flow;
Be our fiery, cloudy Pillar
  All the dreary desert through.
    Strong Deliv'rer!
Be Thou still our Strength and Shield.

3 While we tread this vale of sorrow,
  May we in Thy love abide.
Keep us, O most gracious Saviour!
  Cleaving closely to Thy side,
    Still relying
On The Father's changeless love.

4. Saviour, come, we long to see Thee,
Long to dwell with Thee above,
And to know in full communion
All the sweetness of Thy love.
Come, Lord Jesus,
Take Thy waiting people home.

XXXVIII.—8, 7.

1 Come, Thou Fount of every blessing,
Tune my heart to sing Thy grace:
Streams of mercy never ceasing
Call for ceaseless songs of praise.

2 Teach me, Lord, the rapt'rous measures
Sung by heav'nly hosts above;
While I sing the countless treasures
Of my God's unchanging love.

3 Jesus sought me when a stranger,
Wand'ring from the fold of God;
He to rescue me from danger,
Interpos'd His precious blood.

4 O to grace how great a debtor
Daily I'm constrain'd to be!
Let that grace, Lord, like a fetter,
Bind my wand'ring heart to Thee.

5 Prone to wander, Lord, I feel it;
   Prone to leave the God I love:
Yet Thou, Lord, hast deign'd to seal it,
   With Thy Spirit from above;

6 Rescued thus from sin and danger,
   Purchas'd by the Saviour's blood,
May I walk on earth a stranger,
   As a Son and Heir of God.

XXXIX.—8s.

1 THOUGH twice ten thousand sinners go
   Down to the pit of endless woe,
God's choice, from all repentance free,
   The guard of His elect shall be.

2 To fall from that, if God be true,
   No sinner shall whom He foreknew;
Whom God *will* save, to God *must* rise,
   And fill a mansion in the skies.

3 Triumphant grace shall ever keep,
   The weakest of the way-worn sheep,
Salvation's free and shall be giv'n
   To all who trust the God of Heaven.

XL.—8s.

1 He lives—the great Redeemer lives!
  What joy the blest assurance gives!
  And now, enthron'd above the skies,
  He pleads His Holy sacrifice,

2 Thus has He met our desp'rate case,
  And giv'n us lasting joy and peace;
  The Lamb, Whose life can never end,
  At once our Sacrifice and Friend!

3 Great Advocate, Almighty Friend,
  On Thee do all our hopes depend:
  Our cause can never, never fail,
  For Thou dost plead, and must prevail.

4 In ev'ry dark distressing hour,
  When Sin and Satan join their pow'r,
  Let this bless'd truth repel each dart,
  That Jesus bears us on His heart.

5 Away, then, sad and doubtful thoughts!
  Above our fears, above our faults,
  His pow'rful intercessions rise,—
  And we o'ercome while Satan flies.

XLI.—8, 6.

1 As saints we will not be dismay'd,
    Nor sink in hopeless fear;
For as we ever need His aid,
    The Saviour 's ever near.

2 This Abr'ham found: he rais'd the knife—
    God saw, and said, " Forbear !
You ram shall yield its meaner life,
    Behold the victim there."

3 Once David seemed Saul's certain prey;
    But hark ! the foe's at hand;
Saul turns his arms another way,
    To save th' invaded land.

4 When Jonah sunk beneath the wave,
    He thought to rise no more ;
But God prepar'd a fish to save,
    And bear him to the shore.

5 Since proofs so plain of pow'r and grace,
    Are taught us in His word;
To Fear or Care we 'll not give place,
    But wait upon the Lord.

6 Wait for His seasonable aid,
   And, though it tarry, wait:
The promise may be long delayed,
  · But cannot come too late.

XLII.—6, 6, 8, 6.

1 CHRIST shed His precious blood,
   To make us His alone;
And wash'd in that atoning flood,
   We are no more our own.

2 If He His will reveal,
   Let us obey the call;
Assur'd whate'er the flesh may feel,
   His love deserves our all.

3 Then let us keep in view
   His glory, as our end;
Too much we cannot bear, or do,
   For such a gracious Friend.

4 And let us stand prepar'd
   In duty's path to run;
Nor count the greatest trials hard,
   So that His will be done.

5 With Jesus for our guide,
   The path is safe though rough;
   The Promise says, "I will provide,"
   And Faith replies, "Enough!"

XLIII.—6, 6, 8, 6.

1 WHAT, tho' th' Accuser roar
   Of ills that we have done!
   We know them well, and thousands more,
   Jehovah findeth none.

2 Sin, Satan, Death appear
   To harass and appal;—
   Yet since the gracious Lord is near,
   Backward they go and fall.

3 Before, behind, around,
   They set their fierce array,
   To fight and force us from our ground,
   Along life's narrow way.

4 We meet them face to face,
   Through Jesus' conquest blest;
   March in the triumph of His grace,
   Right onward to our rest.

5 There in His book we bear
 More than a conq'ror's name,
 Of soldier, son, and fellow-heir,
 Who fought and overcame.

XLIV.—SECOND PART.

1 His be "the Victor's name,"
 Who fought our fight alone;
 Triumphant saints no honour claim,
 His conquest was their own.

2 By weakness and defeat,
 He won the meed and crown;
 Trod all our foes beneath His feet,
 By being trodden down.

3 He Hell in hell laid low;
 Made sin, He Sin o'erthrew;
 Bow'd to the grave, destroy'd it so,
 And Death, by dying slew.

4 Bless, bless the Conq'ror slain,
 Slain in His victory;
 Who lived, Who died, Who lives again—
 For thee, His church, for thee!

XLV.—7, 6.

1 O GRACIOUS Shepherd! bind us
  With cords of love to Thee,
And evermore remind us
  How mercy set us free.
O may Thy holy Spirit
  Keep this before our eyes,
That we Thy death and merit
  Above all else may prize!

2 We are of God's salvation,
  Assured through Thy love
Yet, ah! on each occasion,
  How faithless do we prove.
Thou hast our sins forgiv'n—
  Then leaving all behind,
We would press on to heav'n,
  Bearing the prize in mind.

3 Thus may we then, Lord! ever,
  While in this vale of tears,
Look up to Thee, and never
  Give way to anxious fears.
For Thou wilt not forsake us,
  Though we are oft to blame ;
O let Thy love, then, make us
  True to Thy faith and name !

XLVI.—8s.

1 As Debtors to mercy alone,
  Of Heavenly mercy we sing ;
Nor fear, with His righteousness on,
  Our persons and off'rings to bring:
The wrath of a sin-hating God
  With us can have nothing to do:
Our Saviour's obedience and blood
  Hide all our transgressions from view.

2 The work which His goodness began,
  The arm of His strength shall complete:
His promise is Yea and Amen,
  And never was forfeited yet:
Things future, nor things that are now,
  Nor all things below nor above,
Can make Him His purpose forego,
  Or sever our souls from His love.

3 Our names, from the palms of His hands,
  Eternity will not erase ;
Impressed on His heart this remains,
  In marks of indelible grace:
And we to the end shall endure,
  As sure as the earnest is given ;
More happy, but not more secure,
  The souls of the blessed in heav'n.

XLVII.—8, 8, 6. *bis.*

1 O JOYFUL day! O glorious hour!
  When Jesus by Almighty pow'r
    Reviv'd and left the grave;
  In all His works behold Him great,
  Before, Almighty to create,
    Almighty now to save.

2 The first begotten from the dead,
  He 's risen now, His people's head,
    To make their life secure;
  And if like Him they yield their breath,
  Like Him they 'll burst the bonds of death,
    Their resurrection 's sure.

3 Why should His people then be sad,
  None have such reason to be glad
    As those redeem'd to God:
  Jesus, the Mighty Saviour lives,
  To them eternal life He gives,
    The purchase of His blood.

4 Dear Brethren let our praise resound,
  And in His constant work abound,
    Whose blessed name is Love;
  Be sure our labour 's not in vain,
  For we with Jesus yet shall reign,
    With Jesus dwell above.

XLVIII.—8, 7.

1 COME, Thou glorious day of promise!
   Come and spread Thy cheerful ray,
When the scatter'd sheep of Israel
   Shall no longer go astray;
     When Hosannas
   With united voice they'll cry.

2 Lord, how long wilt Thou be angry?
   Shall Thy wrath for ever burn?
Rise! redeem Thine ancient people;
   Their transgressions from them turn:
     King of Israel!
   Come and set Thy people free.

3 O that soon Thou wouldst to Jacob
   Thine enliv'ning Spirit send;
Of their unbelief and mis'ry
   Make, O Lord, a speedy end;
     Lord Messiah!
   Prince of Peace o'er Israel reign,

4 Glory, honour, praise, and power,
   Be unto the Lamb for ever!
Jesus Christ is our Redeemer.
   Hallelujah! Hallelujah!
     Praise ye the Lord.
   Hallelujah! Praise the Lord.

XLIX.—6, 6, 6, 6, 8, 8.

1 By whom was David taught
   To aim the dreadful blow,
   When he Goliah fought,
   And laid the Gittite low?
No sword or spear the stripling took,
But chose a pebble from the brook.

2 'Twas Israel's God and King
   Who sent him to the fight;
   Who gave him strength to sling,
   And skill to aim aright.
Ye feeble saints, your strength endures,
Because young David's God is yours.

3 Who order'd Gideon forth,
   To storm the invader's camp,
   With arms of little worth,
   A pitcher and a lamp?
The trumpets made his coming known,
And all the host was overthrown.

4 But now, while 't is to day,
   Arm'd with the Spirit's sword,
   God helping us to say,
   " Our trust is in the Lord,"
The blood of Christ o'ercomes all foes,
Tho' all the Hosts of Hell oppose.

x

L.—8, 6.

1 For ever blessed be the Lord,
　Our Saviour and our shield;
Who sends His Spirit with His word,
　To arm us for the field.

2 When Sin and Hell their force unite,
　He makes His church His care;
Instructs us for the heav'nly fight,
　And guards us through the war.

3 His help against the hostile Pow'rs
　Doth our weak courage raise;
He makes the glorious vict'ry ours
　Then His shall be the praise.

LI.—8, 6.

1 Let sinners boast of sinful joys,
　The poor delights of sense;
'Tis Christ our inmost thoughts employs,
　We draw our comforts thence.

2 With sweet contentment now we bid
　Farewell to pleasures here;
With Christ in God our life is hid,
　And all its springs are there.

3 'Tis now conceal'd and lodg'd secure
　In God's eternal Son;
From age to age it shall endure,
　Though to the world unknown.

4 Then Lord, remove whate'er divides
　Our lingering souls from Thee;
'Tis fit that where the Head resides
　The members too should be.

LII.—7s.

1 Jesus only—He can give
Peace and comfort while we live;
Jesus only can supply
Boldness if we're call'd to die;
Jesus shall our treasure be,
Through His own eternity:
He is now our nearest Friend,
And His love will never end!

LIII.—8, 7.

1 Happy they who trust in Jesus;
　Sweet their portion is, and sure,
When the foe on others seizes,
　God will keep His own secure.
　　Happy people;
　Happy, though despis'd and poor.

2 Since His love and mercy found us,
 We are precious in His sight;
Thousands now may fall around us,
 Thousands more be put to flight,
  But His presence
 Keeps us safe by day and night.

3 Lo! our Saviour never slumbers,
 Ever watchful is His care;
Though we cannot boast of numbers,
 In His strength secure we are.
  Sweet their portion,
 Who our Saviour's kindness share.

4 As the bird beneath her feathers,
 Guards the objects of her care,
So the LORD His children gathers,
 Spreads His wings and hides them there:
  Thus protected,
 All their foes they boldly dare.

LIV.—8, 7.

1 HARK! ten thousand voices crying
 "Lamb of God!" with one accord;
Thousand thousand saints replying,
 Wake at once th' echoing chord.

2 " Praise the Lamb," the chorus waking,
   All in heav 'n together throng;
Loud and far each tongue partaking
   Rolls around the endless song.

3 Grateful incense this, ascending
   Ever to the Father's Throne ;
Ev'ry knee to Jesus bending,
   All the mind in heav'n is one.

4 All the Father's counsels claiming
   Equal honours to the Son,
All the Son's effulgence beaming,
   Makes the Father's glory known.

5 By the Spirit all pervading,
   Hosts unnumber'd round the Lamb,
Crown'd with light and joy unfading,
   Hail Him as the great " I AM."

6 Joyful now the new creation
   Rests in undisturb'd repose,
Blest in Jesu's full salvation,
   Sorrow now, nor thraldom knows.

7 Hark ! the heavenly notes again !
   Loudly swells the song of praise ;
Throughout creation's vault, Amen !
   Amen ! responsive joy doth raise.

LV.—8, 6.

1 Hosanna to the King of kings!
   The great incarnate Word!
Ten thousand songs and glories wait
   To crown our coming Lord.

2 Thy vict'ries and Thy endless fame
   Through the wide world shall run ;
And everlasting ages sing
   The triumphs Thou hast won.

LVI.—6, 6, 8, 6.

1 Arise, ye saints, arise,
   The Lord our leader is:
The foe before His banner flies,
   For victory is His.

2 Behold, He leads the way !
   We'll follow where He goes,
We cannot fail to win the day
   Since He subdues our foes.

3 Lead on, Almighty Lord,
   Lead on to victory:
Encourag'd by the bright reward,
   With joy we follow Thee.

4 We follow Thee our Guide,
   Who didst salvation bring:
  We follow Thee, through grace supplied
   From heav'n's eternal spring.

LVII.—SECOND PART.

1 We hope to see the day
   When toil and strife shall cease;
  When we shall cast our arms away,
   And dwell in endless peace.

2 This hope supports us here,
   It makes our burdens light;
  It serves our drooping hearts to cheer
   Till faith shall end in sight.

3 Till of the prize possess'd,
   We hear of war no more,
  And, O sweet thought! for ever rest
   On yonder peaceful shore.

LVIII.—7s.

1 FAINT not, Christian! though the road
  Leading to thy blest abode,

Darksome be, and dangerous too,
Christ, thy guide, will bring thee through.

2 Faint not, Christian! though in rage,
Satan doth thy soul engage;
Take thee Faith's anointed shield,
Bear it to the battle field.

3 Faint not, Christian! though the world
Has its hostile flag unfurl'd;
Hold the cross of Jesus fast,
Thou shalt overcome at last.

4 Faint not, Christian! though within,
There's a heart so prone to sin:
Christ the Lord is over all,
He'll not suffer thee to fall.

5 Faint not, Christian! though thy God
Smite thee with the chast'ning rod;
Smite He must, with Father's care,
That He may His love declare.

6 Faint not, Christian! Jesu's near;
Soon in glory He'll appear,
And His love will then bestow,
Victory over ev'ry foe.

7 Faint not, Christian ! look on high,
  Hear the harpers in the sky:
  Patient wait, and thou wilt join,
  Chanting still of love divine.

LIX.—8s.

1 THE saints, of Christ the portion are,
  Redeem'd by grace, reclaim'd by pow'r;
His special choice and tender care,
  Own them, and guard them every hour.

2 He guards them in a barren land,
  Beset with sins, and fears, and woes;
He leads and guides them by His hand,
  And keeps them safe from all their foes.

LX.—8, 7.

1 JESUS, we our cross have taken,
  All to leave, and follow Thee,
All things else for Thee forsaken,
  Thou from hence our all shalt be;
Perish ev'ry fond ambition,
  All we 've sought, or hoped, or known ;
Yet how rich is our condition,
  God and heav'n are still our own.

2 Let the world despise and leave us ;
　　They have left The Saviour too,
　Human hearts and looks deceive us
　　Thou art not, like them, untrue;
　And since Thou dost smile upon us,
　　God of wisdom, love and might,
　Foes may hate, and friends disown us,
　　In Thy love we have delight.

3 Go then, earthly fame and treasure,
　　Come, disaster, scorn, and pain;
　In Thy service, pain is pleasure—
　　With Thy favour, loss is gain—
　We have call'd our God, our Father,
　　We have set our hearts on Thee,
　Storms may howl, and clouds may gather,
　　All must work our liberty.

4 Man may trouble and distress us,
　　'Twill but drive us to Thy breast;
　Life with trials hard may press us,
　　Heav'n will bring us sweeter rest.
　O 'tis not in grief to harm us,
　　With Thy love so full and free,
　O 'twere not in joy to charm us,
　　Were that joy unmix'd with Thee.

LXI.—PART SECOND.

1 CHURCH of God, by Christ's salvation,
    Rise o'er sin, and fear, and care—
Joy to find in ev'ry station,
    Something still to do or bear ;
Think what Spirit dwells within thee—
    Think what Father's smiles are thine—
Think that Jesus died to win thee—
    Bride of Christ! wilt thou repine ?

2 Haste thee on from grace to glory,
    Arm'd by faith, and wing'd by prayer,
Heaven's eternal day 's before thee,
    God's right hand shall guide thee there ;
Soon shall close thine earthly mission,
    Soon shall pass thy pilgrim days,
Hope shall change to glad fruition,
    Faith to sight, and pray'r to praise.

LXII.—8, 6.

1 FATHER of peace, and God of love !
    We own Thy power to save,
That power by which our Shepherd rose
    Victorious o'er the grave.

2 Him from the dead Thou brought'st again
   When, by His sacred blood,
Confirm'd and seal'd for evermore,
   Th' eternal covenant stood.

3 O may the Spirit guide our souls,
   And mould them to Thy will,
That our weak hearts no more may stray,
   But keep Thy precepts still;

4 That to perfection's sacred height
   We nearer still may rise;
And all we think, and all we do,
   Be pleasing in Thine eyes !

LXIII.—8, 6.

1 Sav'd from the awful guilt of sin,
   By Him Who bare the cross ;
We'll now a cheerful strain begin,
   Where God began with us.

2 We sing the vast unmeasur'd grace,
   Of height and depth untold!
Which did the saints elect embrace
   As sheep within the fold.

64

3 We had not known the blood for sin,
   Nor sweets of pard'ning love,
  Unless our worthless names had been
   Enroll'd for life, above.

4 This purpose of eternal love
   Did Jesus' soul sustain;
  And earth or hell, the same to move,
   Did all conspire in vain.

5 Well may we sing, since bought with blood
   Of the Begotten Son;
  O how secure God's purpose stood
   Ere time its race begun!

LXIV.—8, 8, 8, 6.

1 O HOLY Saviour! Friend unseen,
  Since on Thine arm Thou bid'st us lean,
  Help us, throughout life's changing scene,
    By faith to cling to Thee!

2 Blest with this fellowship divine,
  Take what Thou wilt, we'll not repine;
  For as the branches to the vine,
    We only *cling* to Thee!

3 Tho' far from home, fatigu'd, opprest,
   Here we have found a place of rest;
   As exiles still, yet not unblest,
      Because we cling to Thee.

4 Without a murmur we dismiss
   Our former dreams of earthly bliss,
   Our joy, our consolation, this,
      Each hour to cling to Thee.

5 What, though the world deceitful prove,
   And earthly friends and hopes remove;
   With patient uncomplaining love,
      Still can we cling to Thee.

6 Tho' oft we seem to tread alone
   Life's dreary waste, with thorns o'ergrown,
   Thy voice of Love, in gentlest tone,
      Whispers, " Still cling to Me."

7 Though faith and hope are often tried,
   We ask not, need not, aught beside;
   So safe, so calm, so satisfied,
      The souls that cling to Thee.

8 They fear not Satan nor the Grave,
   They know Thee near and strong to save,
   With Thee all danger they can brave,
      Because they cling to Thee.

9 Blest is our lot whate'er befall,
  Who can affright or who appal—
  Since on Thy strength, our rock, our all,
    Jesus ! we cling to Thee.

LXV.—8s.

1 WITH heav'n in view, we tread the path
    The saints of former ages trod ;
  Like them, the children once of wrath,
    But now, like Christ, the sons of God.

2 No room for any boast have we,
    Upon another's wealth we live ;
  The pardon we enjoy is free,
    The praise to God alone we give.

3 We seek a city far from this,
    A distant city, out of sight ;
  Our God Himself its builder is,
    The Lamb, its everlasting light.

4 And sad to us the way appears,
    Till we our Lord and God can see:
  Yet tho' while here we sow in tears,
    Our harvest hence ere long shall be.

5 And yet to us full joy there is,
    In Him Who is the joy of heav'n ;
  And blest our lot ! for we are His !
    Opposers once, but now forgiv'n,

6 Our aim be this, to live below,
   As He would have His people live:
To those who own and serve Him so,
   The Lord a bright reward will give.

LXVI.—8s.

1 THE Church in her militant state
   Is weary, and cannot forbear;
The saints, with desire still wait,
   To see Him again in the air !

2 The Spirit invites in the bride,
   Her Heav'nly Lord to descend ;
And place her, enthron'd at His side,
   In glory that never shall end.

3 The news of His coming I hear,
   And gladly I join in the cry,
O Jesus in triumph appear,
   Appear on the clouds of the sky!

4 Come Lord to the Bride of Thy love,
   In fulness of majesty come ;
And give me the mansion above,
   Prepar'd in Thy heavenly home !

LXVII.—8, 6.

1 JERUSALEM! our heav'nly home
  (Name to us ever dear),
When will the Saviour come, and thou
  To us, His Saints, appear?

2 When shall these eyes thy jasper walls
  And gates of pearl survey;
Thy fabric rear'd on precious stones,
  Of ev'ry brilliant ray.

3 Transparent as the crystal glass,
  And form'd of purest gold;
Perfection's height art thou, of all
  That man can e'er behold.

4 In thee, the myriads of the saints
  Shall in one song unite,
And each the bliss of all shall see
  With infinite delight.

5 O when, thou city of our God,
  Shalt thou for us descend;
And our eternal sabbath come
  When praise shall never end?

LXVIII.—SECOND PART.

1 JERUSALEM! our happy home,
  Our souls still sigh for thee,

Till all our conflicts here are past,
And we Thy glory see.

2 Why should we shrink at pain or woe,
Or feel at death dismay?
Thy matchless glory is in view
And realms of endless day.

3 Apostles, martyrs, saints, shall meet
In Thee (a ransom'd band);
And all who follow Jesus here,
Around Him there shall stand.

4 Then shall His servants serve the Lord,
From sin and sorrow free;
Blest home! thro' rude and stormy scenes
Onward we press to thee.

LXIX.—8, 6.

1 Soon all shall hail our Jesus' name,
Angels shall prostrate fall,
For Him the brightest glory claim,
And hail Him Lord of all.

2 The risen saints shall sound the lyre,
And, as they sound it, fall
Before His face Who formed their choir,
And hail Him Lord of all.

3 The remnant sav'd from Israel's race,
  Redeem'd from Israel's fall,
Shall praise Him for His wondrous grace,
  And hail Him Lord of all.

4 Gentiles shall come—and every king
  Throughout this earthly ball,
To Zion come—and tribute bring,
  And hail Him Lord of all.

5 In Heaven—on earth—shall happy throngs
  In wond'ring rapture fall,
And join in everlasting songs,
  To hail Him Lord of all.

LXX.—6, 6, 6, 6, 8, 8.

1 Jesus, the Lord, is ris'n
    Triumphant o'er the grave;
For us He burst the pris'n,
    Almighty now to save:
Captivity is captive led,
Since Jesus liveth that was dead.

2 Who to our charge shall lay
    Iniquity or guilt?
All sin is done away,
    Since Jesus' blood was spilt.
        Captivity, &c.

3 Who now accuseth them
    Whom God hath justified?
Or who shall those condemn,
    For whom the Surety died?
            Captivity, &c.

4 Christ hath the ransom paid,
    The glorious work is done;
On Him our help is laid,
    The victory is won.
            Captivity, &c.

LXXI.—8, 6.

1 O BLESSED Saviour, is Thy love
    So great! so full! so free!
Behold! we give our thoughts, our hearts,
    Our lives, our all to Thee.

2 We love Thee for the glorious worth
    Which in Thyself we see:
We love Thee for that shameful cross,
    Endur'd so patiently.

3 No man of greater love can boast
    Than for his friend to die;
Thou for Thine enemies wast slain!
    What love with Thine can vie?

4 Though in the very form of God,
    With heav'nly glory crown'd,

Thou didst partake of human flesh,
  Beset with sorrow round.

5 Thou wouldst like wretched man be made
    In ev'ry thing but sin ;
  That we as like Thee might become,
    As we unlike had been.

6 Like Thee in faith, in meekness, love,
    In ev'ry beauteous grace;
  From glory into glory chang'd,
    'Till we behold Thy face.

7 O Lord ! we treasure in our souls
    The mem'ry of Thy love ;
  And ever shall Thy name to us
    A grateful odour prove.

LXXII.—8, 6.

1 The Saint amid this stormy world,
    Is like the flutter'd dove,
  And fain would be as swift of wing,
    To flee to Him we love.

2 The cords that bound our hearts to earth
    Are loos'd by Jesus' hand,
  Before His cross we now are left.
    As strangers in the land.

3 That visage marr'd, those sorrows deep,
    The thorns, the scourge, the gall,
These were the golden chains of love,
    His captives to enthral.

4 Our hearts are with Him on the throne,
    And ill can brook delay,
Each moment longing for that word,
    " Rise up and come away."

LXXIII.—SECOND PART.

1 WITH hope deferr'd, oft faint and sick,
    " Why tarries Christ ?" we cry ;
And if He should rebuke our haste,
    Thus would we make reply ;—

2 " May not the exile, Lord, desire
    Her own sweet realm to see ?
May not the captive seek release ?
    The pris'ner to be free ?

3 " Children, when far away, may long
    For home and kindred dear,
And she that loves her absent Lord,
    Must grieve till He appear."

LXXIV.—THIRD PART.

1 Fain would we, Jesus, know Thy love
    Which yet no measure knows ;

Would search the depth of all Thy wounds,
 The secret of Thy woes.

2 Fain would we strike the golden harp,
 And wear the promis'd crown,
And, at Thy feet while bending low,
 Would sing what Grace has done.

3 Then leave us not in this dark world,
 As strangers long to roam,
Come, Lord, and take us to Thyself,
 Come, Jesus, quickly come!

LXXV.—6, 6, 8, 6.

1 SOLDIERS of Christ, arise,
 And put your armour on—
Strong in the strength which God supplies
 Through His eternal Son.

2 Strong in the Lord of Hosts,
 And in His mighty pow'r—
Who in the strength of Jesus trusts,
 Is more than conqueror.

3 Stand in His heav'nly might,
 With all His strength endu'd,
But take, to arm you for the fight,
 The panoply of God.

4 That having all things done,
   And all your conflicts past,
 Ye may o'ercome, through Christ alone,
   And stand complete at last.

LXXVI.—8, 8, 6, bis.

1 COME on, my partners in distress,
   My comrades thro' the wilderness,
     Who still your sorrows feel;
   Awhile forget your griefs and fears,
   And look beyond this vale of tears,
     To that celestial hill.

2 Look forward to that happy place,
   Beyond the bounds of time and space,
     The Saints' secure abode;
   On faith's strong eagle pinions rise,
   And force your passage to the skies,
     And scale the mount of God.

3 See where the Lamb in glory stands,
   Encircled by His radiant bands,
     And join the angelic pow'rs;
   For all that height of glorious bliss
   Our everlasting portion is,
     And all that heav'n is ours.

4 Who suffer with their Master here,
 Shall soon before His face appear,
  And at His side sit down;
 To patient faith the prize is sure,
 And all who to the end endure
  The cross, shall wear the crown.

5 Thrice blessed, joy-inspiring hope,
 It lifts the fainting spirit up,
  It brings to life the dead;
 Our conflicts here shall soon be past,
 And we shall all ascend at last,
  Triumphant with our Head.

LXXVII.—8s.

1 JESUS, Thy blood and righteousness
 Our beauty are, our glorious dress;
 Midst flaming worlds, in these array'd
 With joy shall we lift up the head.

2 Bold shall we stand in that great day,
 For who aught to our charge shall lay,
 While by Thy blood absolv'd we are
 From sin's tremendous curse and fear?

3 Thus Abraham, the friend of God,
 Thus all the saints redeem'd with blood

Saviour of sinners Thee proclaim,
And all their boast is in Thy name.

4 This spotless robe the same appears,
When ruin'd nature sinks in years,
No age can change its glorious hue,
The robe of Christ is ever new.

5 Then let the dead now hear Thy voice,
And bid Thy chosen ones rejoice,
Their beauty this, their glorious dress,
Jesus, the Lord our righteousness.

LXXVIII.—8, 6.

1 With joy we meditate the grace
    Of our High Priest above;
His heart is fill'd with tenderness,
    His very name is Love.

2 Touch'd with a sympathy within,
    He knows our feeble frame;
He knows what sore temptations mean,
    For He has felt the same.

3 But spotless, innocent, and pure,
    The great Redeemer stood,
While Satan's fiery darts He bore,
    And did resist to blood.

4 He, in the days of feeble flesh,
    Pour'd out His cries and tears,
  And in His measure feels afresh
    What ev'ry member bears.

5 Then boldly let our faith address
    His mercy and His pow'r;
  We shall obtain deliv'ring grace
    In each distressing hour.

LXXIX.—7s.

1 CHILDREN of the heav'nly King,
  As ye journey, sweetly sing;
  Sing the Saviour's worthy praise,
  Glorious in His works and ways.

2 Ye are trav'lling home to God
  In the way the fathers trod;
  Soon, the dead in Christ, and ye
  " With the Lord shall ever be."

3 Shout, ye ransom'd flock and bleat,
  Ye on Jesus' throne shall rest;
  There your seat is now prepar'd,
  There your kingdom and reward.

4 Fear not, though a feeble band,
  Mid the conflict boldly stand:

Jesus Christ, God's own dear Son,
Bids you undismay'd go on.

5 Lord, submissively we go,
Gladly leaving all below;
Only Thou our Leader be,
And we still will follow Thee.

LXXX.—7s.

1 Now begin the heav'nly theme,
Sing aloud in Jesus' name :
Ye, who His salvation prove,
Triumph in Redeeming Love.

2 Ye, who see the Father's grace
Beaming in the Saviour's face,
As to Glory on ye move,
Praise and bless Redeeming Love.

3 Mourning souls, dry up your tears,
Banish all your guilty fears,
See your guilt and curse remove
Cancell'd by Redeeming Love!

4 Welcome, all by sin oppress'd,
Welcome to His sacred rest :

Nothing brought Him from above,
Nothing—but Redeeming Love.

5 He subdu'd th' infernal pow'rs,
Those tremendous foes of ours,
From their boasted empire drove,
Mighty in Redeeming Love.

6 Hither; then, your praises bring,
And of Jesus gladly sing;
Gladly join the hosts above,
Join to praise Redeeming Love.

LXXXI.—8s.

1 ARM of the Lòrd—awake, awake!
The yoke of Judah's bondage break;
Tear from her captive neck the chain
And raise her from the dust again.

2 Awake—as in the days of old,
Bring back the wand'rers to Thy fold.
Shall Israel's sons for ever rove
Far from the house and land they love?

3 O no! before our gladd'ning eyes,
We see the Star of Jacob rise;
The fulness of the isles doth come,
Leading the exil'd people home!

4 They come, they come, on every side,
 To Zion bend, a whelming tide ;
 To Zion bend—no more to stray:
 The veil, the veil is torn away !

5 Peace round them now, where 'er they go,
 Shall like a deep'ning river flow ;
 The conqueror shall conquer'd be,
 And captive led captivity.

LXXXII.—6, 6, 8, 6.

1 COME, ye that love the Lord,
 And let your joys be known ;
 Join in a song with sweet accord,
 And thus approach the throne.

2 Let those refuse to sing
 Who never knew our God ;
 But children should their praises bring,
 And speak their joys abroad.

3 The God who rules on high,
 And all the earth surveys ;
 Who rides upon the stormy sky,
 And calms the roaring seas ;

4 This glorious God is ours—
 A God of boundless love !

And soon He 'll send His heav'nly pow'rs
To carry us above.

5 There we shall see His face,
    And never, never sin ;
There from the fountain of His grace
    Drink endless pleasures in.

6 And now, until we rise
    To that immortal state,
The thoughts of such amazing bliss
    Should constant joy create.

LXXXIII.—8s.

1 MASTER ! we would no longer be
Lov'd by the world that hated Thee,
But patient in Thy footsteps go,
Thy sorrow as Thy joy to know,
We would—and O bestow the pow'r—
With meekness meet the darkest hour,
By shame, contempt, however tried,
For Thou wast scorn'd and crucified.

2 We welcome still Thy faithful word—
"The cross shall meet its sure reward ;"
For soon must pass the "little while,"
When joy shall crown Thy servants' toil:

When we shall hear Thee, Saviour, say
" Arise, my love, and come away;
Look up, for thou shalt weep no more,
But rest on heaven's eternal shore."

LXXXIV.—8, 6.

1 JESUS, in Thee our eyes behold
   A thousand glories more
Than the rich gems and polish'd gold,
   The sons of Aaron wore.

2 They, first, their own sin-offering brought,
   To purge themselves from sin ;
Thy life was pure without a spot,
   And all Thy nature clean.

3 Fresh blood, as constant as the day,
   Was on their altars spilt;
But Thy *one* offering took away
   For ever all our guilt.

4 Thou, great Melchizedec ! shalt reign,
   In peace, on Zion's hill,
(Thyself the Lamb that once was slain),
   And bear Thy priesthood still.

5 Till then for us to intercede
   Before the Father's face,

Be this Thy work, and ours to plead,
Thy merits and His grace.

LXXXV.—8, 7.

1 FLY, ye seasons, fly still faster,
  Let the glorious day come on,
When we shall behold our Master
  Seated on His heav'nly throne;
    When the Saviour
    Shall descend to claim His own.

2 What is earth, with all its treasures,
  To the joy the Gospel brings?
Well may we resign its pleasures,
  Jesus brings us better things;
    All His people
    Draw from heav'n's eternal springs.

3 Fly, ye seasons, fly still faster,
  Swiftly bring the glorious day;
Jesus, come, our Lord and Master,
  Come from heav'n without delay,
    Take Thy people,
    Take, O take them hence away.

LXXXVI.—8, 7.

1 THE night is wearing fast away,
  The day of glory's dawning;

G

When Christ shall all His grace display,
The fair Millennial morning.

2 Gloomy and dark the night has been,
  And long the way, and dreary,
And sad each faithful saint is seen,
  And faint, and worn, and weary.

3 Ye mourning pilgrims! dry your tears,
  And hush each sigh of sorrow;
The light of that bright morn appears,
  The long sabbatic morrow.

4 Lift up your heads—behold from far
  A flood of splendour streaming,
It is the bright and morning Star,
  In living lustre beaming.

5 And see that star-like host around
  Of angel-bands attending:
Hark! hark! the trumpet's gladd'ning sound
  'Mid shouts triumphant blending.

LXXXVII.—SECOND PART.

1 O WEEPING Spouse, arise! rejoice!
  Put off thy weeds of mourning,

And hail the Bridegroom's welcome voice,
  In triumph now returning.

2 He comes! the Bridegroom promis'd long;
  Go forth with joy to meet Him;
And raise the new and nuptial song,
  In cheerful strains to greet Him.

3 Adorn thyself, the feast prepare
  With hallelujahs swelling;
He comes, with thee all joys to share,
  And make this earth His dwelling.

LXXXVIII.—8s.

1 WHY should I fear the darkest hour,
Or tremble at the tempter's pow'r?
Jesus vouchsafes to be my tow'r.

2 Though hot the fight, why quit the field?
Why should I either flee or yield,
Since Jesus is my mighty shield?

3 I know not what may soon betide,
Or how my wants shall be supplied;
But Jesus knows, and will provide.

4 Though sin would fill me with distress,
The throne of grace I can address,
For Jesus is my righteousness.

5 Though faint my prayers, and cold my love,
  My stedfast hope shall not remove
  While Jesus intercedes above.

6 Against me earth and hell combine;
  But on my side is pow'r divine :
  Jesus is all, and He is mine.

LXXXIX.—6, 6, 8, 6.

1 Not all the blood of beasts,
    On Jewish altars slain,
  Could give the guilty conscience peace,
    Or wash away its stain.

2 But Christ, the heavenly Lamb,
    Took all our sins away,—
  A sacrifice of nobler name,
    And richer blood than they.

3 By faith I lay my hand
    On that dear head of Thine,
  While like a penitent I stand,
    And there confess my sin.

4 My soul looks back to see
    The burden Thou didst bear,
  When hanging on th' accursed tree,
    For all my guilt was there.

5 Believing, I rejoice
   To see the curse remove;
And bless the Lamb with cheerful voice,
   And sing Redeeming Love.

XC.—8s.

1 To see the Saviour as He is,
   What can we look for more than this?
Of heav'n 'tis all His people know,
No more is needful here below.

2 A paradise let others feign,
   Where all their fav'rite good obtain,
Where, free from all restraint and fear,
They feast on joys but tasted here.

3 We ask no other heav'n than this,
   To see the Saviour as He is,
To take our place upon His throne,
And know, as we ourselves are known

4 Where Jesus is, 'tis heav'n to be,
   'Tis heav'n the Saviour's face to see;
We know, tho' all the world revile,
Celestial joy is in His smile.

5 The little that on earth we know,
  Makes us impatient hence to go,
  To rise from earth to heav'n above,
  And see the object of our love.

XCI.—10, 10, 11, 11.

1 In Jesus, the Lamb
    (The Father's delight,)
  The Saints without blame,
    Appear in God's sight;
  And while He in Jesus
    Our souls shall approve,—
  So long shall our Father
    Continue His love.

2 In Jesus, free grace
    All blessings secures;
  We know and rejoice
    That all things are ours;
  And God from His purpose
    Will never remove,
  But love us, and bless us,
    "And rest in His love."

XCII.—8, 7.

1 Hark, the notes of angels singing—
  Glory, glory to the Lamb!

All in heav'n their tribute bringing,
  Raising high the Saviour's name.

2 Ye for whom His life was given,
  Sacred themes to you belong,
Come, assist the choir of heaven,
  Join the everlasting song.

3 See the Father hath enthron'd Him,
  At His own right hand on high:
There the heav'nly Hosts have own'd Him,
  Filling with His praise the sky.

4 Fill'd with holy emulation
  Let us vie with those above,
Sweet the theme—a free salvation,
  Fruit of everlasting love.

5 Endless life in Him possessing,
  Let us praise His glorious name,
Glory, honour, pow'r and blessing,
  Be for ever to the Lamb!

XCIII.—8, 6.

1 AWAKE, ye saints, and raise your eyes,
  And raise your voices high;
Extol the sov'reign love, that shews
  Our full redemption nigh.

2 Fast on the wings of time it flies;
   Its coming nought can stay :
It speeds with each revolving year,
   With each declining day.

8 Not many years their rounds shall run,
   Nor many morns shall rise,
Ere all its glories stand reveal'd
   To our admiring eyes.

4 Then let the wheels of nature roll
   Yet onward to decay:
We long to hail the rising sun
   That brings th' eternal day.

XCIV.—8s.

1 JESUS! and shall it ever be,
A mortal man asham'd of Thee !
Asham'd of Thee, Whom angels praise ;
Whose glories shine through endless days !

2 Asham'd of Jesus ! did not He
Give His own life to ransom me ;
And shed the beams of life divine,
O'er this benighted soul of mine ?

Asham'd of Jesus ! that dear Friend,
On Whom my hopes of heav'n depend !

No! when I blush—be this my shame,
That I no more revere His name.

4 Asham'd of Jesus! yes, I may,
When I've no guilt to wash away,
No tear to wipe, no good to crave,
No fears to quell, no soul to save.

5 'Till then—nor is my boasting vain ·
'Till then I boast a Saviour slain!
And O may this my glory be,
That Christ is not asham'd of me!

XCV.—8, 6.

1 WHEN Israel, by divine command,
   The pathless desert trod,
They found, throughout the barren land,
   A sure resource in God.

2 A cloudy pillar mark'd the road,
   And screen'd them from the heat;
From the hard rock the water flow'd,
   And manna was their meat.

3 Like them, we have a rest in view,
   Secure from hostile Pow'rs;
Like them, we pass a desert too,
   But Israel's God is ours.

4 His word a light before us spreads,
   By which our path we see;
His love, a banner o'er our heads,
   From harm preserves us free.

5 Jesus, the bread of life, is giv'n
   To be our daily food;
Himself the wond'rous stream of heav'n,
   The precious grace of God.

6 Lord, 'tis enough, we ask no more;
   Thy grace around us pours
Its rich and unexhausted store,
   And all its joy is ours.

XCVI.—8, 6.

1 Jesus, our Head, once crown'd with thorns,
   Is crown'd with glory now;
Heaven's royal diadem adorns
   The mighty Victor's brow.

2 Delight of all who dwell above,
   The joy of saints below,
To us still manifest Thy love,
   That we its depths may know.

3 To us Thy cross with all its shame,
    With all its grace be giv'n ;
Though earth disowns Thy lowly name,
    All worship it in heav'n.

4 Who suffer with Thee, Lord, below,
    Shall reign with Thee above ;
Then let it be our joy to know
    This way of peace and love.

5 To us Thy cross is life and health,
    Though shame and death to Thee ;
Our present glory, joy, and wealth,
    Our everlasting stay.

XCVII.—7, 9.

1 YES, we hope the day is nigh
    When many nations long enslaved,
Shall break forth, and sing with joy,
    " Hosanna to the Son of David."

2 Abrah'm's seed, cast off so long,
    Shall then appear among the saved,
Shall arise and join the song,
    " Hosanna to the Son of David."

3 Jews and Gentiles shall unite,
    . By Satan's pow'r no more enslaved,

And shall sing with great delight,
"Hosanna to the Son of David."

4 Brighter glory still is nigh,
For Jesus shall collect His saved;
Men and angels then shall cry,
"Hosanna to the Son of David."

XCVIII.—8, 6.

1 COME, saints, your grateful voices raise,
The heav'nly Lamb adore;
Dwell on His everlasting love,
And praise Him evermore.

2 Spread His dear name through all the earth,
Sing His eternal pow'r:
Shout the rich fountain of His blood,
And praise Him evermore.

3 His mercy Who our ransom paid,
And all our sorrows bore,
Sing with a note of loftiest joy,
And praise Him evermore.

4 Soon shall the Lord appear to reign,
Then all from shore to shore
Shall view the glory of the Lamb,
And praise Him evermore.

XCIX.—8, 6.

1 ARE we the soldiers of the cross,
　　The follow'rs of the Lamb?
And shall we fear to own His cause,
　　Or blush to speak His name?

2 Now must we fight, if we would reign;
　　Increase our courage, Lord!
We'll bear the toil, endure the pain,
　　Supported by Thy word.

3 Thy saints, in all this glorious war,
　　Shall conquer though they're slain,
They see the triumph from afar,
　　For they with Thee shall reign.

4 Soon that desired morn shall rise,
　　And all its beauties shine,
And one bless'd song shall rend the skies
　　" The glory, Lord, be Thine!"

C.—6, 6, 8, 6.

1 " FOR ever with the Lord!"
　　Amen, so let it be:
　　Life from the dead is in that word,
　　'Tis immortality.

2 Here in the body pent,
    Absent from Him I roam,
  Yet nightly pitch my moving tent,
    A day's march nearer home.

3 My Father's house on high,
    Home! to my soul how dear;
  I long to see thee, and I sigh
    Within thee to appear!

4 My thirsty spirit faints
    To reach the home I love;
  The bright inheritance of saints,
    Jerusalem above.

5 And though there intervene
    Rough roads and stormy skies,
  Faith will not suffer ought to screen,
    Thy glory from mine eyes.

6 There shall all clouds depart,
    The wilderness shall cease;
  And sweetly shall each gladd'ned heart,
    Enjoy eternal peace.

CI.—SECOND PART.

1 WHILE waiting for the Lord!
  (Mid foes and darkness still)

Truth, light and grace beam from the word,
My soul with joy to fill.

2 A Father's gracious hand,
Whose love can never fail,
Upholds, sustains, and makes me stand,
Whatever foes assail.

3 For Jesus, by His death
Hath rent the veil in twain,
That while I draw this fleeting breath,
I might this blessing gain.

4 Till known as I am known,
Then still this grace afford;
Till I repeat before the throne
"For ever with the Lord.'

CII.—6, 6, 8, 6.

1 Though in a foreign land,
We are not far from home;
And nearer to our rest above,
We ev'ry moment come,

2 Secure within the veil,
Christ is our anchor strong;
While pow'r supreme, and love divine,
Still guide us safe along.

3 And should the surges rise—
   Should sore afflictions come—
Blest is the sorrow, kind the storm,
   That brings us nearer home.

4 God's grace will to the end
   Clearer and brighter shine;
Nor present things, nor things to come,
   Can change His love divine.

5 Soon shall our pains and fears
   For ever pass away;
For we shall soon the Saviour see
   In everlasting day.

CIII.—8, 7.

1 SHEPHERD of the chosen number,
   They are safe whom Thou dost keep;
Other shepherds faint and slumber,
   And forget to guard the sheep.
     Watchful Shepherd!
   Thou dost wake while others sleep.

2 When the Shepherd's life was needful
   Or the sheep must else be lost,
Not of Thine own safety heedful,
   But of their's alone, Thou wast:
     Thou didst save them;
   But no tongue can tell the cost!

CIV.—7s.

1 GLORY unto Jesus be!
From the curse Who set us free;
All our guilt on Him was laid,
He the ransom fully paid.

2 All His blessed work is done,
God's well pleased in His Son,
For He rais'd Him from the dead,
Set Him over all as Head.

3 All should sing His work and worth,
All above, and all on earth,
As they sing around the throne,
"Thou art worthy, Thou alone."

4 Ye who love Him, cease to mourn,
He will certainly return,
All His saints with Him shall reign,—
"Come, Lord Jesus, come! Amen."

CV.—6, 6, 8, 6.

1 GRACE is the sweetest sound
That ever reach'd our ears!
When conscience charg'd and justice frown'd,
'Twas grace remov'd our fears.

2 'Tis freedom to the slave,
  'Tis light and liberty ;
It takes its terror from the grave,
  From death its victory.

3 Grace is a mine of wealth
  Laid open to the poor ;
Grace is the sov'reign spring of health ;
  'Tis LIFE FOR EVERMORE.

4 This grace then let us sing !
  (O joyful, wondrous theme !)
Who *grace* has brought, shall *glory* bring,
  And we shall reign with Him.

5 Then shall we see His face
  With all the saints above,
And sing for ever of His grace,
  For ever of His love.

CVI.—8, 6.

1 THE King of kings and Lord of lords
  Shall soon with clouds descend,
And the last trumpet's awful voice
  The heav'ns and earth shall rend.

2 Then they who live shall changed be,
 And they who sleep shall wake ;
The grave shall yield its prisoners,
 And earth's foundations shake.

3 The saints of God, from death set free,
 With joy shall mount on high ;
The Lord is come—and gladly they
 Shall meet Him in the sky.

4 Together to their Father's house,
 With joyful hearts they go ;
And dwell for ever with the Lamb,
 Beyond the reach of woe.

5 A few short years of evil past,
 We reach the happy shore,
Where death-divided friends at last
 Shall meet, to part no more.

CVII.—8s.

1 Away with our sorrow and fear !
 We soon shall have enter'd our home ;
The city of saints shall appear,
 The day of eternity come !

111

Men, once, like us, with suff'ring tried,
  Now resting till they're crown'd!

3 Behold a Witness nobler still,
    Affliction's path Who trod;
  Jesus, our Leader and Reward,
    Our Saviour and our God.

4 He, for the joy before Him set,
    (So boundless was His love,)
  Endur'd the cross, despis'd the shame,
    And now He sits above.

5 If He unnumber'd griefs and wrongs
    With meekness did sustain,
  O how can we, whose sins He bore,
    Of lighter ills complain!

CXI.—8, 7.

1 NOTHING but Thy blood, O Jesus,
    Could relieve the sinner's smart;
  Nothing else from guilt release us,
    Nothing else could melt the heart.

2 Sense of sin doth only harden
    All the while it works alone;
    t the grace that seals our pardon,
    ;oon dissolves a heart of stone.

CXII.—8s.

Jesus! before Thy face we fall,
Our Lord, our life, our hope, our all;
For we have no where else to flee;
No Sanctuary, Lord, but Thee.

2 In Thee we ev'ry glory view,
Of safety, strength, and beauty too;
'Tis all our rest and peace to see
Our Sanctuary, Lord, in Thee.

3 Whatever foes or fears betide,
In Thy dear presence let us hide;
And while we rest our souls on Thee,
Do Thou our Sanctuary be.

4 Through time, with all its changing scenes
And all the grief that intervenes,
Let this support each fainting heart,
That Thou our Sanctuary art.

CXIII.—8s.

1 The Cross! the Cross! O that's our gain,
Because on that the Lamb was slain;
'Twas there the Lord was crucified,
'Twas there for us the Saviour died.

2 What wondrous cause could move Thy heart,
To take on Thee our curse and smart,
Well knowing we should ever be
So cold, so negligent of Thee !

3 The cause was love,—we sink with shame
Before our blessed Jesu's name ;
That He should bleed and suffer thus,
Because He lov'd and pitied us.

CXIV.—8, 6.

1 SAVIOUR divine, Whose name we know,
In Whom alone we trust,
Thou art the Lord our Righteousness,
Thou art Thy people's boast.

2 The soul, by sin howe'er defil'd,
By guilt howe'er opprest,
In Thee believing, stands approv'd,
And finds abiding rest.

3 To Thee, our great redeeming Lord,
What lasting thanks we owe,
For raising sinners to such joys,
From depths of endless woe !

CXV.—8s.

1 AWAKE, each saint, in joyful lays,
To sing thy great Redeemer's praise;
He justly claims a song from thee:
His loving-kindness, O how free!

2 He saw thee ruin'd in the fall,
Yet lov'd thee, notwithstanding all;
He sav'd thee from thy low estate:
His loving-kindness, O how great!

3 Though num'rous hosts of mighty foes,
Though earth and hell its way oppose;
He safely leads His church along:
His loving-kindness, O how strong!

4 When trouble, like a gloomy cloud,
Has gather'd thick, and thunder'd loud:
He with His Church has always stood:
His loving-kindness, O how good!

5 Soon shall we mount and soar away,
To the bright realms of endless day;
And sing with rapture and surprise,
His loving-kindness in the skies.

CXVI.—7s.

1 GREAT the joy when Christians meet;
Christian fellowship how sweet!
When, their theme of praise the same,
They exalt Jehovah's name !

2 Sing ye then eternal love,
Such as did the Father move:
He beheld the world undone ;
Lov'd the world, and gave His Son.

3 Sing the Son's unbounded love;
How He left the realms above ;
To rejoin the Father's side
With a blood-bought spotless Bride.

4 In the love too, make your boast,
That vouchsaf'd the Holy Ghost,
He has chas'd the mists away,
Turn'd our night to glorious day.

5 Sweet the thought, exceeding sweet !
We shall soon in glory meet,
There to raise a sweeter strain,
Of redeeming love again.

CXVII.—8s.

1 MAY we, O God ! Thy mind express,
Stand forth Thy chosen witnesses;
Thy pow'r unto salvation shew,
In love and holiness below.

2 The fulness of Thy grace receive,
And simply to Thy glory live ;
Strongly reflect the light divine,
And in a world of darkness shine.

3 In us let all mankind behold
How Christians liv'd in days of old,
Mighty their envious foes to move,
A proverb of reproach—and love.

4 O make us of one soul and heart,
The all-conforming mind impart,
And grant us peace and unity !
As taught, renew'd, and rul'd by Thee.

CXVIII.—8, 6.

1 O GOD, our languid hearts inspire,
(For here we know Thou art);
And freely of Thy heav'nly fire,
To every soul impart.

2 For Jesus' sake, we pray Thee, here
   Thy presence now display;
  As Thou hast giv'n a place for pray'r,
   So give us faith to pray.

3 Amongst us, Lord, let holy peace,
   And love, and concord dwell;
  And give each troubl'd conscience ease,
   Each wounded spirit heal.

4 May we in faith receive Thy word,
   In faith present our prayer;
  And in the bosom of our Lord
   Cast off our ev'ry care.

CXIX.—8, 7.

1 PEACE be to this congregation,
   Peace to ev'ry Saint therein,
  Peace, the foretaste of salvation;
   Peace, the fruit of pardon'd sin,
  Peace, that speaks its heav'nly Giver—
   Peace to worldly minds unknown,
  Peace divine, that flows for ever
   From its source, the Lord alone!

2 Prince of Peace, be ever near us,
   Till Thou take us to Thy home!

Till Thy bright appearing cheer us,
 Till Thy peaceful kingdom come!
Deign,—with sweetest consolation,
 Deign to give our souls to prove
All the pow'r of Thy salvation,
 Full submission, faith, and love!

CXX.—8, 7.

1 Look, ye saints, look there and wonder!
 See the place where Jesus lay:
He has burst the bands asunder;
 He has borne our sins away.
  Joyful tidings!
 Yes, the Lord is ris'n, we say.

2 Jesus triumph'd! Sing ye praises;
 By His death He overcame:
Thus the Lord His glory raises;
 Thus He fills His foes with shame.
  Sing ye praises!
 Praises to the Victor's name.

CXXI.—8, 7.

1 Look, ye saints,—the sight is glorious,—
 See "the Man of Sorrows" now,

121

From the fight returned victorious,
  Ev'ry knee to Him doth bow.
Crown Him! Crown Him!
  Crowns become the Victor's brow.

2 Crown the Saviour! Angels, own Him!
  Rich the trophies Jesus brings;
In the seat of pow'r enthrone Him,
  While the vault of heaven rings,
Crown Him! Crown Him!
  Crown the Saviour, "King of kings!

3 Sinners in derision crown'd Him,
  Mocking thus the Saviour's claim:
Saints and angels, crowd around Him,
  Own His title, praise His name;
Crown Him! Crown Him!
  Spread abroad the Victor's fame,

4 Hark! those bursts of acclamation:
  Hark! those loud triumphant chords!
Jesus takes the highest station,
  O what joy the sight affords!
Crown Him! Crown Him!
  "King of kings, and Lord of lords!"

CXXII.—8, 7.

1 Soon shall Israel, long dispersed,
  Mourning, seek the Lord their God;
Look on Him Whom once they pierced,
  Own and kiss the chast'ning rod.

2 Then all Isr'el shall be saved,
  War and tumult then shall cease;
While the Blessed Son of David
  Rules a conquer'd world in peace.

3 Zion's King shall reign victorious,
  All the earth shall own His sway;
He will make His kingdom glorious,
  And shall reign through endless day.

CXXIII.—6, 6, 8, 6.

1 Grace! 'Tis a charming sound,
  Harmonious to the ear;
Heav'n with the echo shall resound,
  And all the earth shall hear.

2 Grace taught our wand'ring feet
  To tread the heav'nly road;
And new supplies, each hour we meet,
  While walking thus with God.

124

3 'Twas Grace that wrote each name
   In Life's eternal book;
'Twas Grace that gave us to the Lamb
   Who all our sorrows took.

4 Grace sav'd us from the foe,
   Grace taught us how to pray;
And God will ne'er His grace forego,
   Till we have won the day.

5 May Grace, free Grace, inspire
   Our souls with strength divine;
May all our thoughts to God aspire,
   And Grace in service shine.

CXXIV.—6, 6, 6, 6, 8, 8.

1 YOUR praises hither bring,
   Your Lord, ye saints, adore;
Let us give thanks and sing,
   And triumph evermore.
Lift up your hearts, lift up your voice,
Rejoice aloud, ye saints, rejoice.

2 With Christ our theme begins
   The Lord of truth and love,
When He had purg'd our sins
   He took His seat above.

Lift up your hearts, lift up your voice
Rejoice aloud, ye saints, rejoice.

3 His kingdom cannot fail,
    He'll rule o'er earth and heav'n,
The keys of death and hell
    To Him alone are giv'n.
Lift up your hearts, lift up your voice
Rejoice aloud, ye saints, rejoice.

4 Rejoice in glorious hope:
    Jesus, the Lord, shall come,
And take His brethren up
    To their eternal home.
Lift up your hearts, lift up your voice,
Rejoice, again we say, rejoice.

CXXV.—7s.

1 LORD, accept our feeble song!
Pow'r and praise to Thee belong;
We would all Thy grace record,
Holy, holy, holy Lord!

2 Rich in glory, Thou didst stoop,
Thence is all Thy people's hope;
Thou wast poor, that we might be
Rich in glory, Lord, with Thee.

128

The hope of glory, Christ, is thine,
A child of glory thou.

2 Thy spirit through the lonely night,
From earthly joy apart,
Hath sigh'd for one that's far away,
The Bridegroom of thy heart.

3 But see, the night is waning fast,
The breaking morn is near,
And Jesus comes with voice of love,
Thy drooping heart to cheer.

4 He comes—for O His yearning heart
No more can bear delay,
To scenes of full unmingled joy
To call His Bride away.

5 This earth, the scene of all His woe,
A homeless wild to thee,
Full soon upon His heav'nly throne
Its rightful King shall see.

6 Thou too shalt reign—He will not wear
His crown of joy alone,
And Earth His royal Bride shall see
Beside Him on the throne.

7 Then weep no more, 'tis all thine own,
His crown, His joy divine,
And sweeter far than all beside,
He, He Himself is thine.

CXXIX.—8, 6.

1 A PILGRIM through this lonely world
The blessed Saviour pass'd,
A mourner all His life was He,
A dying Lamb at last.

2 That tender heart that felt for all,
For all its life-blood gave;
It found on earth no resting-place,
Save only in the grave.

3 Such was our Lord—and shall we fear
The cross with all its scorn?
Or love a faithless evil world
That wreath'd *His* brow with thorn?

4 No—facing all its frowns or smiles,
Like Him, obedient still,
We homeward press through storm or calm,
To Zion's blessed hill.

5 In tents we dwell amid the waste,
  Nor turn aside to roam
In folly's paths, nor seek our rest
  Where *Jesus* had no home.

6 Dead to the world with Him Who died
  To win our hearts—our love,
We, risen with our risen Head,
  In spirit dwell above.

7 By faith His boundless glories there
  Our wond'ring eyes behold,
Those glories which eternal years
  Shall never all unfold.

8 This fills our hearts with deep desire
  To lose ourselves in love,
Bears all our hopes from earth away,
  And fixes them above.

CXXX.—8, 6.

1 'Tis come—the glad millennial morn!
  The Son of David reigns—
Sing, sing, O earth! for thou art free,
  And Satan is in chains—

2 Rejoice, for thou shalt feel no more
   The ruthless tyrant's rod,
Nor lose again the gracious smile
   Of thine incarnate God.

3 But chiefly thou, O Solyma!
   Thou queen of cities, sing,
With shouts of triumph welcome now
   The morning-star, thy King.

4 He, gracious Saviour, faithful still
   To thee, His faithless dove,
Forgives thee all, and bids thee dwell
   Within His breast of love.

5 Nor thee alone, for see, on high
   His Saints triumphant now,
With all the hosts of Seraphim,
   In ceaseless worship bow.

6 On Him the happy myriads there
   Unwearied love to gaze,
There He amid His brethren dwells,
   The Leader of their praise.

7 Oh blessed Lord! we little dream'd
   Of such a morn as this!
Such rivers of unmingled joy,
   Such full unbounded bliss.

8 And O how sweet the happy thought!
   That all we taste or see,
We owe it to the dying Lamb,
   We owe it all to Thee.

9 Yes, dearest Saviour, one with Thee,
   Sweet source of joy divine!
With Thee we live, with Thee we reign,
   And we are wholly Thine.

CXXXI.—9s.

1 WE are not come to the burning brow,
Whence the fiery streams of vengeance flow,
To the voice of words, and the trumpet-sound,
Where the prostrate hosts lay quaking round ;

2 But we are come to the angels' abode,
That numberless wait round the throne of God,
To the church of the first-born enroll'd on high,
And the spirits of saints who no more may die;

3 And we are come to the sprinkled shrine,
Where Justice and Mercy unitedly shine,
And the still, small voice of the blood that shed
It's blessing on the murderer's head:

4 'Tis "PEACE" to us our God thus speaks,
Before His vengeance in thunder breaks ;

He shall shake the skies, the seas and the shore,
He shall shake them once, and shall shake no
    more.

CXXXII.—8, 6.

1 AWAKE, ye saints, arise! too long
    In heaviness we sing,
  'Tis time to raise a gladlier song,
    And strike a louder string;

2 In faith we wait for that dear place
    The lov'd Apostle view'd,
  When full before his ravish'd gaze,
    The Holy City stood.

3 Lo! where the pearly gates unfold,
    A kingly, priestly train;
  With robes of white, and crowns of gold,
    Ascend with Christ to reign!

4 No moon, in borrow'd glory bright,
    No Sun, remotely fair;
  Jehovah-Jesus is the light,
    Their joy—The Lord is there!

5 God of the new Jerusalem,
    From Thee this glory flows,

Be ours the grace that prosper'd them,
And ours the same repose.

CXXXIII.—8s.

1 FATHER of Glory, we would know
The richest gifts Thine hands bestow;
The hope of our high calling see,
And scan our immortality.

2 Th' exceeding greatness of Thy pow'r
To us-ward who believe, secure,
The depths of love Thy wisdom plann'd,
The works and wonders of Thy hand.

3 This was the power in Jesus wrought,
When from the dead the Son was brought,
Then set at God's right hand on high,
Above all principality.

4 Above dominion, might, and name,
Of noblest rank, or widest fame,
In this our earthly, fading home,
Or worlds, or kingdoms yet to come.

5 Thus to the Son were all things given,
All for the Church, the Bride of heaven,
Jehovah-Jesus' meet abode,
The fulness of th' unbounded God.

CXXXIV.—8, 7.

1 SAVIOUR, haste! our souls are waiting
For the long expected day,
'When, new heav'ns and earth creating,
Thou shalt banish grief away,
All the sorrow,
Caus'd by sin and Satan's sway.

2 Haste! O hasten Thine appearing!
Take Thy mourning people home:
'Tis this hope our spirits cheering,
While we in the desert roam,
Makes Thy people
Strangers here, till Thou dost come.

3 Lord, how long shall the creation
Groan and travail sore in pain;
Waiting for its sure salvation,
When Thou shalt in glory reign,
And like Eden,
This sad earth shall bloom again?

4 Gather, too, Thy chosen nation,
Israel's long afflicted race;
Let them find Thy free salvation,
Own and trust Thy wondrous grace,
And adoring,
Look on Thy once marred face.

5 Reign, O reign, Almighty Saviour!
   Heav'n and earth in one unite;
Make it known, that in Thy favour,
   There alone is life and light:
     When we see Thee,
   We shall have unmix'd delight.

CXXXV.—7, 6.

1 O Lord! Who now art seated,
   Above the Heav'ns on high,
(The gracious work completed,
   For which Thou cam'st to die);
To Thee our hearts are lifted,
   While pilgrims wand'ring here,
For Thou alone art gifted
   Our ev'ry weight to bear.

2 We know that Thou hast bought us,
   And wash'd us in Thy blood;
We know Thy grace has brought us,
   As kings and priests to God.
We know that soon the morning,
   Long look'd-for hast'neth near,
When we, at Thy returning,
   In glory shall appear.

CXXXVI.—SECOND PART.

1 O Lord, Thy love's unbounded!
   So full, so vast, so free!
Our thoughts are all confounded
   Whene'er we think of Thee:
For us Thou cams't from Heav'n,
   For us to bleed and die;
That purchas'd and forgiven,
   We might ascend on High.

2 O let this love constrain us
   To give our hearts to Thee:
Let nothing henceforth pain us,
   But that which paineth Thee.
Our joy, our one endeavour—
   Thro' suff'ring, conflict, shame,—
To serve Thee, gracious Saviour,
   And magnify Thy name.

CXXXVII.—8, 8, 6.

1 Hark! how the blood-bought hosts above,
Conspire to chaunt the Saviour's love,
   In sweet harmonious strains!
And while they strike their golden lyres,
This glorious theme each bosom fires,
   That Grace triumphant reigns!

2 We'll join the song! for we can tell
How sov'reign grace dissolv'd the spell,
  That kept us bound in chains;
And from that dear and happy day,
How oft, by grace constrain'd to say
  That Grace triumphant reigns!

3 For tho' we 've stray'd like saints of old,
Grace has restor'd us to the fold
  As captives in its chains;
Thus, sav'd by grace, we 'd gladly sing,
Till all the Heav'ns and earth should ring
  With "*Grace triumphant reigns!*"

4 Grace still,—till all redeem'd by blood
Are taught to know themselves and God,—
  Its empire shall maintain;
To spoil the mighty of the prey,
And set the captive exile free,
  Shall Grace triumphant reign.

5 Then,—call'd to meet the church's Head,
The Saviour's grace shall banish dread,
  His love our souls sustain;
And, as we rise to endless day,
We 'll raise the voice, and boldly say,
  Grace doth triumphant reign!

CXXXVIII.—8s

1 Jesus, Thou glorious Priest and King,
Accept the tribute which we bring;
Accept each feeble song of praise,
Which here on earth Thy saints may raise.

2 May every minute as it flies,
Increase our love, improve our joys;
Till we are brought to sing Thy name
At the great supper of the Lamb.

3 O that the months would roll away,
And quickly bring the marriage-day;
When Thou the Lamb shalt take Thy throne
And fully there the Church shalt own.

4 The gladness of that happy day,
In this sad world's our strength and stay—
Then let not faith forsake its hold,
Lest comfort sink, and love grow cold.

CXXXIX.—8, 6.

1 HARK, the glad sound! the Saviour comes!
The Saviour promis'd long!
Take up the word, ye saved saints,
Renew the gladsome song.

2 He comes! creation to release
   In Satan's bondage held;
The Tyrant's thraldom to destroy,
   And make th' Usurper yield.

3 He comes! the mighty foe to bind,
   The groaning earth to free;
While (chief of all free grace's gifts)
   Himself its Lord shall be.

4 Our glad hosannas, Prince of Peace,
   Thy welcome shall proclaim;
And all creation shall rejoice
   In Thy beloved name.

CXL.—8, 6.

1 How sweet the name of Jesus sounds
   In a believer's ear!
It soothes his sorrows, heals his wounds,
   And drives away his fear.

2 It makes the wounded spirit whole,
   And calms the troubled breast;
'Tis manna to the hungry soul,
   And to the weary rest.

3 Dear name! the rock on which I build,
   My shield and hiding-place;
   My never-failing treas'ry, fill'd
   With boundless stores of grace.

4 Jesus, my Shepherd, Saviour, Friend,
   My Prophet, Priest, and King;
   My Lord, my Life, my Way, my End,
   Accept the praise I bring.

5 Weak is the effort of my heart,
   And cold my warmest thought;
   But when I see Thee as Thou art,
   I'll praise Thee as I ought.

6 Till then I would Thy love proclaim
   With ev'ry fleeting breath;
   And triumph in that blessed name
   Which quells the power of Death.

CXLI.—8s.

1 Jesus, the Christ! eternal Word!
   Of all creation Sovereign Lord!

K

On Thee alone, by faith we rest ;
And lean our weakness on Thy breast.

2 Thy blood hath wash'd us from our sin ;
Thy Spirit sanctifies within !
And Thou for us, in all our need,
At God's right hand dost ever plead.

3 O keep us in the narrow way,
That ne'er from Thee our footsteps stray :
Sustain our weakness ; calm our fear ;
And to Thy presence keep us near.

4 And be it thus till that blest day,
When God shall wipe all tears away.
" Quickly "—'tis promis'd in the word ;
E'en so.   Amen.   Come quickly, Lord !

CXLII.—8, 6.

1 HOPE of our hearts! O Lord, appear,
Thou glorious Star of day !
Shine forth, and chase the dreary night,
With all our tears, away.

2 Strangers on earth, we wait for Thee :
O leave the Father's throne ;

Come, with a shout of vict'ry, Lord,
And claim us as Thine own.

3 O bid the bright archangel, then,
The trump of God prepare,
To call Thy saints—the quick—the dead—
To meet Thee in the air.

4 No resting place we seek on earth,
No loveliness we see;
Our eye is on the royal crown
Prepar'd for us and Thee.

5 But O the thought of sharing, Lord,
Thy glorious throne above,
What is it to the *brighter* hope
Of dwelling in Thy love?

6 What to the joy—the *deeper* joy,
Unmingled, pure, and free,
Of union with our living Head,—
Of fellowship with Thee?

7 This joy e'en now on earth is our's;
But only, Lord, above,

    Thy saints, without a pang, shall know
      The fulness of Thy love.

8 There, near Thy heart, upon the throne,
    Thy ransom'd Bride shall see
What grace was in the bleeding Lamb,
    Who died to make her free.

CXLIII.—8, 7.

1 BRIGHT with all His crowns of glory
    See the royal Victor's brow;
Once for sinners marr'd and gory—
    See the Lamb exalted now,
      While before Him
    All His ransom'd brethren bow.

THE CHURCH.

2 Blessed morning! long expected,
    Lo, they fill the peopled air,
Mourners once, by man rejected,
    They, with Him, exalted there,
      Sing His praises,
    And His throne of glory share.

ISRAEL.

3 Judah! Lo thy royal Lion
   Reigns on earth, a conqu'ring King,
Come, ye ransom'd tribes! to Zion,
   Love's abundant off'ring bring;
      There behold Him,
      And His ceaseless praises sing.

THE GENTILES.

4 King of kings! let earth adore Him,
   High on His exalted throne.
Fall, ye nations, fall before Him,
   And His righteous sceptre own;
      All the glory
      Be to Him, and Him alone!

CXLIV.—8, 6.

1 O BLESSED Jesus! who but Thou,
   On earth, in heav'n above,
May claim from all our willing hearts
   The full response of love?

2 We love the brethren, Lord, 'tis true,
   But O in them we see
Sweet traces of Thy blessed self,
   For they are one with Thee.

3 And one with us—but O 'twas thine
  Thine only, Lord, to part
With life, and all that love could give,
  To win the wand'ring heart.

4 Thus, heirs of endless bliss with Thee,
  We love Thee—we adore—
Ah! give us all still greater grace
  To love Thee more and more!

CXLV.—6, 6, 8, 6.

1 SINCE Christ and we are one,
  Why should we doubt or fear?—
He sits upon the Father's throne,
  And in Him we are there.

2 The Spirit doth unite
  Our souls to Him our Head,
And forms us to His image bright
  While we His footsteps tread.

3 And grace it is—free grace—
  Which keeps us on the road,
Till we behold the Saviour's face.
  And city of our God.

CXLVI.—8, 6.

1 ALL things that God or man could wish,
  In Jesus richly meet;
 Not to our eyes is light so dear,
  Or friendship half so sweet.

2 O may His Name still cheer our hearts,
  And shed its fragrance there!
 The sweetest balm of ev'ry wound,
  The cure of ev'ry care.

CXLVII.—8, 7.

1 BRIGHTNESS of the Father's glory,
  Shall Thy praise unutter'd lie?
 Who would hush the boundless story,
  Of the Lamb Who came to die;

2 Came from off the throne eternal,
  Down to Calv'ry's depth of woe,
 Came to crush the pow'rs infernal?—
  Streams of praises ceaseless flow!

3 Sing the Lamb's triumphant rising;
  Sing Him on the Father's throne;

Sing—till heav'n and earth surprising,
Reigns the Nazarene alone.

CXLVIII.—8, 6.

1 SEE ! See, the blessed Saviour comes
  The God of love and grace ;
With Him we spend eternity
  In pleasure and in praise.

2 For ever still our wond'ring eyes
  Shall o'er His beauties rove ;
To endless ages we adore
  The wonders of His love !

CXLIX.—8, 7.

1 I'M glad I know that Christ shall reign
  In glory, glory, glory,
And come to earth on clouds again,
  With glory, glory, glory :
'Tis glory's foretaste makes me sing
  Of glory, glory, glory,
And to the Saviour praises bring ;
  Sing glory, glory, glory !

2 I hope to see Him on His throne,
    Sing glory, glory, glory!
When He shall come to meet His own,
    In glory, glory, glory!
I'll sing, while mounting through the air,
    Of glory, glory, glory!
And meet my Father's children there,
    In glory, glory, glory!

3 Come on, my friends, let's mend our pace
    To glory, glory, glory!
For we shall see Him face to face,
    In glory, glory, glory!
The Bride shall reign—the Bridegroom too,
    In glory, glory, glory!
Let's keep the blessed prize in view:
    'Tis glory, glory, glory!

CL.—8, 6.

1 THE God Who dwells above, we call
    Our Father and our Friend:
And, blessed thought! His children all
    Shall see Him in the end.

2 Though now dispers'd, the day will come
    When He Who made us His,

Will take us hence, and bear us home
To see Him as He is.

3 Though now unknown, we then shall be
The sons of God confess'd;
Those Who disown us then shall see
That we alone are bless'd.

4 Then let us, brethren, while on earth,
With foes and strangers mix'd,
Be mindful of our heav'nly birth,
Our thoughts on glory fix'd.

5 That we should glorify Him here
Our Father's purpose is;
And when the Saviour shall appear,
He will declare us His.

CLI.—6, 6, 8, 6.

1 Not to ourselves we owe
That we, O God, are Thine;
Jesus, the Sun, our night broke through,
And gave us light divine.

152

2 The Father's grace and love,
   This blessed mercy gave,
And Jesus left the throne above,
   The wand'ring sheep to save.

3 No more the heirs of wrath,—
   The smile of peace we see;
And, Father, in confiding faith,
   We cast our souls on Thee.

4 We drink the living stream
   To all Thy children giv'n,
The love which Thou hast made to beam
   From Christ, the Heir of Heaven.

5 With the adopted band,
   Soon shall we see Thee there;
With them and Him in glory stand,
   And all His honours share.

CLII.—8s.

1 It hath not fully yet appear'd
   What blessedness to saints is giv'n;
No eye hath seen, no ear hath heard,
   No heart conceiv'd the joy of heav'n.

2 The mind of God, and it alone,
    The joy prepar'd hath understood ;
  When saints shall know as they are known,
    And shall behold the face of God—

3 The face of Him, Who here below
    Appear'd, and died to save His own ;
  The same Who dwells in glory now,
    And sits upon the Father's throne.

4 The sight of Him His saints shall fill
    With transport never known before ;
  They 'll feel no want, and fear no ill,
    Nor sin nor sorrow any more.

5 Then blest our lot ! for we are His,
    And we shall dwell with Him above ;
  Yea, we shall see Him as He is,
    The Lord of grace, of truth, and love.

CLIII.—8s.

1 WHEN will the trumpet loud proclaim
  The judgment of the martyr'd Lamb ?
  When will the captive saints be free,
  And keep th' eternal jubilee ?

2 O Father, let that day appear,
   The promis'd Great Sabbatic Year;
   When freed from sin, and toil, and pain,
   Thy ransom'd shall in glory reign.

3 Till then we cannot let Thee rest,
   But still repeat our strong request.
   And this our constant cry shall be,
   Lord, sound the trump of jubilee.

CLIV.—8s.

1 AND art Thou, gracious Master, gone,
      A mansion to prepare for me?
   Shall I behold Thee on Thy throne,
      And there for ever sit with Thee?
   Then let the world approve or blame,
   I'll triumph in Thy glorious name.

2 Should I, to gain the world's applause,
      Or to escape its harmless frown,
   Refuse to countenance Thy cause,
      And make Thy people's lot mine own,
   What shame would fill me in that day
   When Thou Thy glory shalt display!

3 No; let the world cast out my name,
      And vile account me, if they will;

If to confess my Lord be shame,
  I purpose to be viler still;
For Thee, my God, I'd all resign,
Content that I can call Thee mine.

4 For ah! what joy will fill my heart,
  ' When Thou my worthless name shalt own,
When I shall see Thee as Thou art,
  And know as I myself am known:
When I, from sin and sorrow free,
Shall like my Lord for ever be.

CLV.—6, 6, 6, 6, 8, 8.

1 Ye watchful saints, arise!
  Quick, from the dead awake!
Unto salvation wise,
  Oil in your vessels take;
Awake! and hear the midnight cry,
"Behold the heav'nly Bridegroom nigh."

2 He comes, He comes to call
  The nations to His bar,
And raise to glory all
  Who call'd to glory are;
Make ready for your full reward,
And go with joy to meet your Lord.

3 To meet Him in the sky,
   Your everlasting Friend ; —
Your Head to glorify,
   With all His saints,—ascend ;
There see the Saviour face to face.
   And sing for ever of His grace.

4 Brethren, this is our hope
   (Let it to all be known),
That we shall be caught up
   To share the Saviour's throne,
Call'd to partake the marriage feast,
Though of all saints the very least.

5 Then let us wait to hear
   The trumpet's welcome sound ;
That when the Lord appear,
   Watching may we be found !
Cloth'd in the righteousness divine,
In which His Bride shall ever shine.

CLVI.—8s.

1 WE sing the praise of Him Who died,
   Of Him Who died upon the cross,
The sinner's Hope—let men deride ;
   For this we count the world but loss.

2 Inscrib'd upon the cross we see,
  In shining letters, "God is Love!'
The Lamb Who died upon the tree;
  Has brought us mercy from above.

3 The Cross! it takes our guilt away,
  It holds the fainting spirit up;
It cheers with hope the gloomy day,
  And sweetens ev'ry bitter cup.

4 It makes the coward spirit brave,
  And nerves the feeble arm for fight;
It takes its terror from the grave,
  And gilds the bed of death with light.

5 The balm of life, the cure of woe,
  The measure and the pledge of love,
The sinners' refuge here below,
  The angels' theme in heav'n above.

CLVII.—8, 8, 6. bis.

1 O Thou Who didst Thy glory leave,
  Apostate sinners to retrieve
    From nature's deadly fall;
  As Thou hast bought us with a price,
  Our sins against us ne'er can rise,
    For Thou hast borne them all.

2 We sing One smitten in our stead,
Him Who without the city bled
    To expiate our stain ;
Who, God of God, vouchsaf'd to dwell
In flesh, to make of full avail
    The suff'rings of the man.

3 See Him for our transgressions giv'n,
See the incarnate God of heav'n,
    For us, His foes, expire ;
Rejoice ! rejoice ! the tidings hear !
He bore, that we might never bear,
    His Father's righteous ire.

4 Ye saints, " the Man of sorrows" bless,
The Lord, for your unrighteousness
    Deputed to atone ;
Praise, till with all the ransom'd throng
Ye sing the never-ending song,
    And sit upon His throne !

CLVIII.—8s.

1 YES ! 'tis a rough and thorny road
That leads us to the saints' abode ;
But when our Father's house we gain,
'Twill make amends for all our pain.

2 And though we feel our present grief,
In hope we find a sweet relief ;

L

For hope anticipates the day,
When all our grief shall pass away.

3 And what is all we suffer now,
Or all we can endure below,
To that bright day when Christ shall come,
And take His weary pilgrims home?

4 Then let us tread, without complaint,
The thorny road, and never faint;
Though now by weariness opprest,
The end is everlasting rest.

CLIX.—7, 6.

1 O Head! so full of bruises,
    So full of pain and scorn,
'Midst other sore abuses
    Mock'd with a crown of thorn;
O Head! e'en now surrounded
    With brightest majesty,
In death once bow'd and wounded,
    Accursed on the tree.

2 Thou Countenance transcendent!
    Thou life-creating Sun
To worlds on Thee dependent,
    Yet bruis'd and spit upon.
O Lord! what Thee tormented
    Was our sin's heavy load,

We had the debt augmented,
　Which Thou didst pay in blood.

3 When sealing our election
　Thy heart did break in woe,
With shame and love's affection,
　That men should treat Thee so;
We know Thy love's strong fervour
　By all Thy pain and grief;
Then hear us, Great Preserver,
　And worship now receive.

CLX.—SECOND PART.

1 WE give Thee thanks unfeigned,
　O Jesus! Friend in need,
For what Thy soul sustained,
　When Thou for us didst bleed;
Grant us to lean unshaken
　Upon Thy faithfulness;
Until to glory taken,
　We see Thee face to face.

2 And O what consolation
　Doth in our hearts take place,
While we Thy toil and passion
　Do joyfully retrace!
Ah! should we, while thus musing
　On our Redeemer's cross,

E'en life itself be losing,
Great gain would be that loss.

CLXI.—6, 6, 8, 6.

1 O Saviour, we are Thine
In everlasting bands;
Our names, our hearts, we would resign
Into Thy gracious hands.

2 To Thee we now would cleave
With firm and faithful zeal,
Though often press'd Thy paths to leave,
Oh let not sin prevail!

3 Our lives we'd gladly lose
As not our own but Thine;
For Thee the tempter's wiles refuse,
And all the world resign.

4 Let nothing from us hide
The glory of Thy day,
But keep us ever near Thy side
Through all life's gloomy way.

5 Since Thou and we are one,
We know we need not fear;
If Thou in heav'n hast fix'd Thy throne
We too are fixed there.

CLXII.—8, 6.

1 LET us rejoice in Christ the Lord,
　　Who claims us for His own;
　The hope that's built upon His word,
　　Can ne'er be overthrown.

2 Though many foes beset us round,
　　And feeble is our arm,
　Our life is hid with Christ in God
　　Beyond the reach of harm.

3 Weak as we are, we shall not faint,
　　Or, fainting, cannot fail;
　Jesus, the strength of ev'ry saint,
　　Must in the end prevail.

4 Though now He's unperceiv'd by sense,
　　Faith sees Him always near,—
　A guide, a glory, a defence,
　　To save from ev'ry fear.

5 As surely as He overcame,
　　And conquer'd death and sin,
　So surely those that trust His name
　　Will all His triumph win.

CLXIII.—8s.

1 GREAT Saviour of the church, we own
   Thy precepts all divinely wise;
O may Thy mighty pow'r be known,
   To keep them all before our eyes.

2 Deep on our hearts Thy word engrave,
   And fill our breasts with heav'nly zeal,
That while we trust Thy Love to save,
   We may Thy sacred word fulfil.

3 Adorn'd with ev'ry heav'nly grace,
   May we in service brightly shine;
And the full glory of Thy face
   Reflected beam from each of Thine.

4 That lovely image, true and fair,
   Our heav'nly Father shall proclaim;
And men that see its brightness there,
   Shall join to glorify His name.

5 Of truth the pillar and the ground,
   May we continue all our days;
In love and discipline be found,
   As truly witnessing His praise.

CLXIV.—8, 6.

1 THE Son of God, Who once for us
   Did to the grave descend,
Now lives in heav'n, our great High Priest,
   And never-dying friend.

2 Through life or death let us to Him
   With constancy adhere;
Faith shall supply new strength, and hope
   Shall banish ev'ry fear.

CLXV.—8, 8, 6 bis.

1 HE bids us come; His voice we know,
   And boldly on the waters go,
     To Him our God and Lord;
We walk on life's tempestuous sea,
For He Who died to set us free
     Hath call'd us with His word.

2 Secure, on boist'rous waves we tread,
   Nor all the billows round us dread,
     While to the Lord we look;
The Tempter drives his vortex round;
We pass it as on solid ground;
     The wave is firm as rock.

3 But if from Him we turn the eye,
   We see the raging floods run high,
      We feel our fears within ;
   Our foes so strong, our flesh so frail,
   Reason and unbelief prevail,
      And plunge us into sin.

4 Lord ! we our unbelief confess,
   Do Thou our little faith increase,
      That we may doubt no more ;
   But fix on Thee a steady eye,
   And on Thine outstretch'd arm rely,
      Till all the storm is o'er.

CLXVI.—8, 7.

1 FATHER, we commend our spirits
      To Thy love in Jesu's name,
   Love, which His atoning merits
      Give us confidence to claim.

2 O how sweet, how real a pleasure
      Flows from love so true and free!
   O how great, how rich a treasure,
      Saviour, we possess in Thee!

3 From the world and its confusions
      Here we turn and find our rest,

From its care and its delusions,
Turn to Thee, and there are blest.

4 Though this scene is ever changing,
Since Thy mercy changes not,
O'er the waste our spirits ranging
Glory in their happy lot.

5 By the Holy Ghost anointed,
May we do our Father's will,
Walk the path by Him appointed,
Jesu's pleasure to fulfil.

6 Till the welcome signal hearing,
Welcome to the saints alone,
We rejoice at His appearing,
Who shall claim us for His own.

CLXVII.—8.

1 FROM far we see the glorious day,
When He Who bore our sins away,
Will all His majesty display.

2 "A Man of Sorrows" once He was,
No friend was found to plead His cause,
For all preferr'd the world's applause.

3 He groan'd beneath sin's awful load,
  For in the sinner's place He stood,
  And died to bring us back to God.

4 But now He sits with glory crown'd,
  While angel hosts the throne surround,
  And still His lofty praises sound.

5 To few on earth His name is dear;
  And they who in His cause appear,
  The world's reproach and scorn must bear.

6 Yet soon there is a day to come,
  When He will seal the scorner's doom,
  And take His mourning people home.

7 Jesus, Thy name is all our boast
  And though by waves of trouble tost,
  Thou wilt not let Thine own be lost.

8 Come then, come quickly from above,
  Our souls impatient long to prove
  The depths of Thine eternal love.

CLXVIII.—8, 6.

1 GREAT Leader of the church of God,
  We sing Thy conqu'ring name,

Legions of foes beset Thee round,
 But all were put to shame.

2 A vict'ry, glorious and complete,
 Thou by Thy death didst gain;
So in Thy cause would we contend,
 And all for Thee sustain.

3 While onward to the conflict led,
 No sorrow would we fear, .
Prepar'd our ransom'd lives to shed,
 Nor count them to us dear.

4 We 'd trace the footsteps Thou hast trod
 To glory and renown;
Sustain Thy combat and Thy cross, .
 As call'd to share Thy crown.

CLXIX.—8, 6.

1 BRETHREN, awake, awake from sloth!
 And bind the girdle on;
A heav'nly course before you lies,
 And an eternal crown.

2 'Tis Jesu's animating voice
 That calls you from on high,

'Tis His own hand presents the prize—
The crown of victory.

3 Lord! help us still to follow Thee,
Patient, the race to run,
Till crown'd with vict'ry round Thy Throne,
We sing what grace has done.

CLXX.—6, 6, 8, 6.

1 THE promise is fulfill'd,
Salvation's work is done;
Justice and Mercy reconcil'd,
For God has rais'd His Son.

2 He left death's sad abode,
From all corruption free;
The holy, harmless, Son of God
Could no corruption see.

3 In Him the saints are ris'n,
From guilt and judgment clear,
And now upon the throne of heav'n,
In Him their Head appear.

CLXXI.—8s.

1 How blest the bright morning appears,
When Jesus reviv'd from the grave!

To banish for ever our fears,
  To triumph, almighty to save.
How strong were His tears and His cries!
  The worth of His blood how divine!
How perfect His one sacrifice,
  Who rose, though He suffer'd for sin!

2 The Man, Whose mock-crown was of thorn,
  Whom sinners agreed to deride,
The Man, Who bore scourging and scorn,
  The Man, Who on Calvary died,
Now blessed for ever is made,
  And life has rewarded His pain;
Now glory encircles His head,
  Heav'n sings of the Lamb that was slain.

3 And lo! when He cometh again,
  His foes shall be clothed with shame;
But gladness the saints shall obtain,
  And glory, and peace, with the Lamb.
Then let us look forward to this,
  And joyfully take up His cross:
As saints we shall be where He is,
  And all that we lose is but dross.

CLXXII.—6, 6, 6, 6, 8, 8.

1 WHO is the wondrous King,
　　Who there in glory stands?
What *title* doth He bring,
　　That *worship* He demands?
Jehovah's name, in battle strong,
Alone can be the Church's song.

2 The pow'rs of hell oppos'd,
　　When He in conflict bled;
And death's strong bars were clos'd
　　Round His expiring head:—
But death and hell possess'd no pow'r,
To hold *Him* past th' appointed hour.

3 'Twas for the church He bled,
　　'Twas for the Church He rose,
That she in Him, her Head,
　　Might overcome all foes:—
Jehovah Jesus is His name,
And all His deeds His worth proclaim.

4 Himself the Son of God,
　　The Lord, from conquest come;
He shed His precious blood,
　　That we might share His home.

Gladly we own His *title*, then,
And at His feet in *worship* bend.

CLXXIII.—8, 6.

1 For Sion's sake I will not rest;
I will not hold my peace,
Until Jerusalem be blest,
And Judah dwell at ease.

2 Until her righteousness return,
As day-break after night;
The lamp of her salvation burn
With everlasting light.

3 The Gentiles shall her glory view,
And kings declare her fame,
And hers shall be a title new,
Which Israel's God shall name.

4 The Lord shall hold her with His hand,
And wear her for His own,
His diadem her beauteous land,
Her royalty His crown.

5 And ev'ry tribe, and ev'ry land,
Shall hear the joyful word,

" The holy people are at hand,
" Redeemed of the Lord."

CLXXIV.—6, 6, 6, 6, 8, 8.

1 THE day comes on apace,
   Soon shall the night be past:
Who trust the Saviour's grace
   Shall see His face at last;
The clouds that now obstruct their sight,
Shall quickly all be put to flight.

2 Ye saints, lift up your heads,
   Salvation draweth nigh;
See where the morning spreads
   Its radiance through the sky;
O let the sight your spirits cheer !
The Lord Himself will soon appear.

3 Though men your Hope deride
   (Nor will e'en God believe),
Do you in Him confide,
   Whose word can ne'er deceive;
When heav'n and earth shall pass away,
The saints shall see a glorious day.

4 For you the Lord intends
   A bright abode on high,

The place where sorrow ends,
  And nought is known but joy;
With such a hope, ye saints, rejoice,
Ye soon shall hear th' archangel's voice.

CLXXV.—7, 6.

1 THE day of glory bearing
  Its brightness far and near,
The day of Christ's appearing
  We now no longer fear;

2 He once a spotless victim
  For us on Calv'ry bled ;
Jehovah did afflict Him,
  And bruis'd Him in our stead.

3 But now He's interceding
  For us who on Him rest ;
And grace from Him proceeding,
  Tells us in Him we're blest.

4 Then let Him come in glory,
  Who comes His saints to raise,
To perfect all the story
  Of wonder, love, and praise.

M

CLXXVI.—8, 7.

1 HERE we rest,—in wonder viewing
   All our sins on Jesus laid !
And a full redemption flowing
   From the sacrifice He made.

2 Truly blessed is the station !
   Thus upon the Lamb to rest,
And to know in God's salvation,
   How the saints are fully blest.

3 Here we find the dawn of heaven,
   While upon the Lamb we gaze,
See our trespasses forgiven,
   And our songs of triumph raise.

4 Oh ! that strong in faith abiding,
   We may to the Saviour cleave,
Nought with Him our hearts dividing,
   All for Him content to leave.

5 May we still, God's mind discerning,
   To the Lamb for wisdom go ;
There new wonders daily learning,
   All the Father's glory know.

CLXXVII.—8, 7.

1 Jesus, lead us by Thy power
    Safe into the promis'd rest ;
  Choose the path ;—the way whatever
    Seems to Thee, O Lord ! the best;
  Be our guide in ev'ry peril,
    Watch and keep us night and day,
  Else our foolish hearts will wander
    From the straight and narrow way.

2 Since in Thee we found redemption,
    And Salvation full and free,
  Nothing can our souls dishearten
    But forgetfulness of Thee ;
  Nought can stay our steady progress,
    More than conq'rors we shall be,
  If our eye, whate'er the danger,
    Looks to Thee, and none but Thee.

3 In Thy presence we are happy ;
    In Thy presence we 're secure ;
  In Thy presence all afflictions
    We can easily endure ;

In Thy presence we can conquer,
  We can suffer, we can die ;
Wand'ring from Thee we are feeble ;
  Let Thy love, then, keep us nigh.

CLXXVIII.—6, 6, 8, 6.

1 From Egypt lately freed,
    By the Redeemer's grace,
  A rough and thorny path we tread
    To see Him face to face.

2 The promis'd rest and peace
    Are still in constant view ;
  How diff'rent to the wilderness
    We now are passing through !

3 Here grief, and care, and pain,
    And fears distress us sore ;
  But there celestial pleasures reign,
    And we shall weep no more.

CLXXIX.—8s.

1 "We 've no abiding city here ;"
    This may distress the worldling's mind,
  But should not cost the saint a tear,
    Who hopes a better rest to find.

2 " We 've no abiding city here;"
   Sad thought! were this to be our home;
But let this truth our spirits cheer,
   We seek a city yet to come.

3 " We 've no abiding city here;"
   Then let us live as pilgrims do;
Let not the world our rest appear,
   But let us haste from all below.

4 " We 've no abiding city here;"
   We seek a city out of sight,
Jerusalem! faith sees it near,
   Brilliant with everlasting light.

CLXXX.—8, 6.

1 CHILDREN of God! who, pacing slow,
   Your pilgrim path pursue,
In strength and weakness, joy and woe,
   To God's high calling true!

2 Why move ye on with ling'ring tread,
   A doubtful, mourning band?
Why faintly hangs the drooping head?
   Why drops the feeble hand?

3 O! weak to know the Saviour's pow'r,
    To trust the Father's care;
A moment's toil, a passing show'r,
    Is all the grief ye share !

4 The Lord of light, absent awhile
    Shall soon His glory bring,
And you in all that glory smile,
    Whilst you His praises sing.

5 Then rescu'd from the gloomy shroud
    Which doth this world invest,
He'll raise you on His glorious cloud,
    And guide you to His rest.

CLXXXI.—7s.

1 SWEETER sounds than music knows,
    Charm us in the Saviour's name;
All the Church's gladness flows
    From His birth, and cross, and shame.

2 Did the Lord a man become,
    That He might the law fulfil?
Bleed and suffer in our room?
    And can any tongue be still?

3 No, we will our praises bring,
 Though they worthless are and weak;
For, should we refuse to sing,
 Sure, the very stones would speak.

4 O our Saviour! shield and sun,
 Shepherd, brother, husband, friend,
Ev'ry precious name in one,
 We would praise Thee without end.

CLXXXII.—8s.

1 WE long to behold Him array'd
 With glory and light from above,
The Lord in His beauty display'd,
 The beauty of holiest love.
We hasten and sigh to be there,
 Where Jesus shall fix His abode,
To see Him descend in the air,
 With all the bright glory of God.

2 With Him we on Zion shall stand,
 (For Jesus hath spoken the word)—
And all of Immanuel's land,
 Survey in the sight of the Lord.

But when on His bosom reclin'd,
  His face we are strengthen'd to see,
Our joyfulness, Lord, we shall find,
  Our heaven of heavens in Thee.

CLXXXIII.—6, 6, 8, 6, 4, 7.

1 From Egypt lately come,
  Where death and darkness reign,
We seek our new, our better home,
  Where we our rest shall gain:
    Hallelujah!
We are on our way to God.

2 To Canaan's sacred bound
  We haste with songs of joy,
Where peace and liberty are found,
  And sweets that never cloy;
    Hallelujah! &c.

3 There sin and sorrow cease,
  And ev'ry conflict's o'er;
There we shall dwell in endless peace,
  And never hunger more.
    Hallelujah! &c.

4 There in celestial strains,
  Enraptur'd myriads sing,

There love in every bosom reigns,
  For God Himself is king;
    Hallelujah, &c.

5 We soon shall join the throng;
  Their pleasures we shall share,
And sing the everlasting song,
  With all the ransom'd there;
    Hallelujah, &c.

6 How sweet the prospect is!
  It cheers the pilgrim's breast;
We're journeying through the wilderness,
  But soon shall gain our rest;
    Hallelujah! &c.

CLXXXIV.—8s.

1 WHEN I behold the wondrous cross
  On which the Lord of glory died,
My richest gain I count but loss,
  And pour contempt on all my pride.

2 Forbid it, Lord, that I should boast,
  Save in the death of Christ, my God;
All the vain things that charm'd me most,
  I'd sacrifice them to His blood.

3 By suffering there, beneath His feet
    He trod the fierce Avenger down ;
There, power itself and weakness meet,
    Emblems of each yon thorny crown !

4 Were the whole realm of nature mine,
    That were an off'ring far too small ;
Love so amazing, so divine,
    Demands my soul, my life, my all.

CLXXXV.—6, 6, 6, 6, 8, 8.

1 On earth the song begins ;
    In heav'n more sweet and loud,
"To Him that cleans'd our sins
    By His atoning blood ;"
"To Him," we sing in joyful strain,
"Be honour, pow'r, and praise, Amen."

2 Believers now repeat,
    What heav'n with gladness owns;
And while before His feet
    The elders cast their crowns,
Come, imitate the choirs above,
And sing aloud the Saviour's love.

3 Alone He bore the cross,
   Alone its grief sustain'd ;
His was the shame and loss,
   And He the vict'ry gain'd ;
The mighty work was all His own,
Tho' we shall share His glorious throne.

CLXXXVI.—8, 8, 6, bis.

1 COME let us sing the matchless worth,
And sweetly sound the glories forth
   Which in the Saviour shine,
To God and Christ our praises bring ;
The song with which the heavens ring,
   Now let us gladly join.

2 How rich the precious blood He spilt,
Our ransom from the dreadful guilt
   Of sin against our God ;
How perfect was His righteousness,
In which unspotted beauteous dress,
   His saints have ever stood !

3 How rich the character He bears,
And all the form of love He wears,
   Exalted on the throne ;

In songs of sweet untiring praise,
We would, to everlasting days,
Make all His glories known.

4 And soon the happy day shall come,
When we shall reach our destin'd home,
And see Him face to face;
Then with our Saviour, Brother, Friend,
The one unbroken day we'll spend
In singing still His grace.

CLXXXVII.—6, 6, 6, 6, 8, 8

1 JOIN all the glorious names
Of wisdom, love, and pow'r,
That mortals ever knew,
That angels ever bore;
All are too mean to speak His worth,
Too mean to set the Saviour forth.

2 Great Prophet of our God!
Our tongues must bless Thy name,
By Whom the joyful news
Of our salvation came;
The joyful news of sins forgiv'n,
Of hell subdu'd, of peace with heav'n.

3 Thou art our Counsellor,
    Our Pattern, and our Guide,
And Thou our Shepherd art;
    Ah, keep us near Thy side;
Nor let our feet e'er run astray,
Or wander in the crooked way.

4 We love Thy well-known voice,
    And trust Thine eye to keep
Our wand'ring souls among
    The thousands of God's sheep;
Feed Thou His flock, call Thou their names,
And gently lead the tender lambs.

CLXXXVIII.—SECOND PART.

1 Should all the hosts of death,
    And pow'rs of hell unknown,
Put their most dreadful forms
    Of rage and mischief on,
We shall be safe, while Christ displays
His guardian and Almighty grace.

2 O Thou Almighty Lord!
    Hell's conqueror and King,
Thy sceptre and Thy sword,
    Thy love and grace we sing;

Thine is our pow'r, and we would sit, ::
In willing bonds, close at Thy feet.

3 Yet, help us now to rise,
   And tread the tempter down ;
O Jesus, lead us forth
   To conquest, and the crown;
And feeble saints shall win the day,
Though death and Hell obstruct the way.

CLXXXIX.—7s.

1 JESUS, Saviour of the soul,
   Let us to Thy bosom fly,
While the raging billows roll,
   While the tempest still is high;
Hide us, O our Saviour, hide,
   Till the storm of life is past:
Safe into the haven guide,
   There receive Thy church at last.

2 Other refuge have we none,
   Helpless, hanging still on Thee ;
Leave, O leave us not alone,
   Still our stay and comfort be;
All our trust on Thee is stay'd,
   All our help from Thee we bring ;
Cover each defenceless head
   With the shadow of Thy wing.

3 Thou, O Lord, art all we want,
    Boundless love in Thee we find ;
Raise the fallen, cheer the faint,
    Heal the sick, and lead the blind.
Just and holy is Thy name,
    We are all unrighteousness ;
We are full of sin and shame
    Thou art full of truth and grace.

4 Plenteous grace with Thee is found
    Grace to pardon ev'ry sin ;
Let the healing streams abound,
    Make and keep us pure within.
Thou of life the fountain art,
    Freely let us take of Thee ;
Spring Thou up within each heart,
    Rise to all eternity.

CXC.—8, 6.

1 Since Thou, the everlasting God,
    Our Father art become ;
Jesus, our Guardian and our Friend,
    And heav'n our final home ;

2 We welcome all Thy sov'reign will
    For all Thy will is love ;

And when we know not what Thou dost,
We wait the light above.

3 Thy gracious love in all our need
Shall heav'nly light impart ;
And be our theme of endless praise,
When all things else depart.

CXCI.—7s.

1 CHRIST deliver'd me when bound,
And, when wounded, heal'd my wound,
Sought me wand'ring, set me right,
Turn'd my darkness into light.

2 Can a mother's tender care
Cease toward the child she bare ?
Yes, she may forgetful be,
Yet will He remember me.

3 His is an unchanging love,
Higher than the heights above,
Deeper than the depths beneath,
Free and faithful, strong as death.

4 I shall see His glory soon,
When the work of grace is done,

Partner of His throne shall be ;
Such His wondrous love to me !

5 This alone is my complaint,
That my love is weak and faint ;
Yet I love Him, and adore,
O for grace to love Him more !

CXCII.—7s.

1 HAPPY christian, God's own child,
Chosen, call'd, and reconcil'd ;
Once a rebel full of taint,
Now a duteous, humble saint.

2 Happy christian, look on high,
See thy portion in the sky ;
Fix'd by everlasting love,
Who that portion can remove ?

3 Happy christian, though the earth
Cannot know thy gracious worth,
Yet thy God shall soon proclaim,
Through all heav'n, thy favour'd name.

4 Happy christian, angels say,
" Turn thy heart from earth away,

N

193

Leave the world and all its woes,
Take with Christ thy sweet repose."

5 Happy christian, onward fly,
Rise, the kingdom now is nigh!
When thou shalt, upon His throne,
See what Christ has made thine own.

CXCIII.—8s.

1 O Jesus, to tell of Thy love
Our souls shall for ever delight,
And join with the blessed above ‒
In praises by day and by night.
Wherever we follow Thee, Lord,
Admiring, adoring, we see
That love which was stronger than death,
Flow out without limit, and free.

2 Descending from glory on high,
With men Thy delight was to dwell,
Contented, our surety to die,
By dying to save us from hell;
Enduring the grief and the shame,
And bearing our sin on the cross,
Oh! who would not boast of this love,
And count the world's glory but loss?

CXCIV.—8, 6.

1 THY gracious presence, O, our God;
   Our ev'ry wish contains;
With this, beneath temptation's load,
   The heart no more complains.

2 This can our ev'ry care control,
  . ˙Gild each dark scene with light;
This is the sunshine of the soul:
   Without it all is night.

3 O happy scenes of pure delight,
   Where Love's full beams impart
Unclouded beauty to the sight,
   And gladness to the heart.

4 Our place in those fair realms of bliss,
   Our spirits long to know;
Our wishes terminate in this,
   Nor can they rest below.

5 Nor do these wishes of the heart
   Seem foolish, Lord, to Thee;
For thou hast said, that where Thou art,
   There we shall ever be.

6 Thus can our cheerful spirits sing
    The darkest hour away,
And rise on faith's expanded wing,
    To everlasting day.

CXCV.—7, 6.

1 O Jesus Christ, the Saviour,
    We only look to Thee;
'Tis in Thy love and favour
    Our souls find liberty.
While Satan fiercely rages,
    And shipwreck oft we fear,—
'Tis this our grief assuages
    That *Thou* art always near.

2 Yes, tho' the tempest round us
    Seems safety to defy;
Tho' rocks and shoals surround us,
    And swell the billows high—
Thou dost from death protect us,
    And cheer us by Thy love;
Thy counsels too direct us
    Safe to the Rest above.

3 There—with what joy reviewing
    Past conflicts, dangers, fears,—

Thy hand our foes subduing,
  And drying all our tears,—
Our hearts with rapture burning,
  The path we shall retrace,
Where now our souls are learning
  The riches of Thy grace.

4 O then how loud the chorus
  Shall to Thy name resound,
From all at rest before us,
  From all Thy grace hath found!
One joyful song for ever
  Each harp, each lip shall raise,
The praise of our Redeemer,
  Our God and Saviour's praise.

CXCVI.—7, 6.

1 How long, O Lord our Saviour,
  Wilt Thou remain away?
Our hearts are growing weary
  Of Thy so long delay;
O when shall come the moment,
  When, brighter far than morn,
The sunshine of Thy glory
  Shall on Thy people dawn?

2 How long, O gracious Master,
  Wilt Thou Thy household leave?
So long hast Thou now tarried,
  Few Thy return believe:
Immers'd in sloth and folly,
  Thy servants, Lord, we see;
And few of us stand ready
  With joy to welcome Thee.

3 How long, O Heav'nly Bridegroom,
  How long wilt Thou delay!
And yet how few are grieving,
  That Thou dost absent stay:
Thy very Bride her portion
  And calling hath forgot,
And seeks for ease and glory
  Where Thou, her Lord, art not.

4 O wake Thy slumbering virgins;
  Send forth the solemn cry,
Let all Thy saints repeat it,
  "The Bridegroom draweth nigh!"
May all our lamps be burning,
  Our loins well girded be,
Each longing heart preparing
  With joy Thy face to see.

CXCVII.—8, 7.

1 ONCE we all were wretched strangers,
  All the enemies of God ;
Heedless of our sins and dangers,
  On the brink of death we stood,
    Nought deserving
  But of wrath the fiery flood.

2 *Now* our blinded eyes are waking,
  And our misery we see ;
Now our stony hearts are breaking ;
  From eternal wrath we flee
    To the refuge,
  Open'd, Lamb of God, in Thee.

3 'Twas Thy Love, O God, that knew us
  Earth's foundation long before:
That same love to Jesus drew us
  By its sweet constraining pow'r,
    And will keep us
  Safely now, and evermore.

4 God of love, our souls adore Thee !
  We would still Thy grace proclaim,
Till we cast our crowns before Thee,
  And in glory praise Thy name ;
    Hallelujah !
  Be to God and to the Lamb.

CXCVIII. — 6, 6, 6, 6, 8, 8.

" No man ever yet hated his own flesh, but nourisheth
and cherisheth it, even as the Lord the Church." Eph.
v. 28, 29.

1 WHEN first, in purpose deep,
   The Church was brought to view,
In God's eternal mind,—
   (Though none His counsel knew),
The Father gave her to the Son,
And He betroth'd her for His own.

2 And though in Adam's loins
   She brake His holy word;
And, treach'rously untrue,
   Departed from her Lord:
He brought her back, though hell withstood,
Wash'd from her sins in His own blood.

3 Part of that church are we,—
   Whom He did thus redeem,
Learning by daily proof
   Our daily need of Him;
Taught by the Spirit to confess
Jesus our only righteousness.

4 Yea, more,—to crown the whole
   (His gracious plan to prove),

Our union, found in Christ,
  Nor earth nor hell can move;
Our daily boast and song is this—
Jesus is ours, and we are His.

5 Yes! we are one with Him
  'Mid all our lep'rous state;
And who was ever yet
  Fain his own flesh to hate?
"One spirit with the Lord!" this proves—
In loving us Himself He loves.

6 Nor can He cease to love;
  For His own precept is,
"Ye husbands love your wives,"—
  And will not Christ love His?
Will not He cherish and refresh
Bone of His bone, flesh of His flesh?

7 Ah, yes! Christ loves the church
  'Tis her He lives to bless;
He cannot love her more,
  Nor will He love her less:
Fair in His sight, cleans'd by the word,
A bride adorn'd, meet for her Lord.

CXCIX.—7s.

1 THRO' the Holy Ghost it is,
Christ is ours, and we are His;
Earth and hell in vain combine,
To dissolve this tie Divine.

2 Since we are the Father's care;
None beside need we to fear,
Us to Jesus He hath giv'n,
Sons of God, and heirs of Heav'n.

3 In His death we met our doom,
He our Shepherd is become;
Strong in His full strength we stand,
None can pluck us from His hand.

4 In this Shepherd's love secure,
To the end we shall endure,
In His service onward go,
Till we conquer ev'ry foe.

CC.—6, 6, 8, 6.

1 THE person of the Lamb,
Enfolding ev'ry grace,
Once slain, but now alive again,
In Heav'n demands our praise.

2 Gladly of Him we sing,
    Since we with Him are dead;
Our life is hid with Christ in God,
    In Christ the Church's Head.

3 A heav'nly calling this!
    It sounds thro' earth abroad;
For we, by faith, in HEAV'N behold
    The kingly priest of God.

CCI.—7s.

1 JESUS, spotless Lamb of God,
    Thou hast bought us with Thy blood—
We would value nought beside
Jesus—Jesus crucified.

2 We are Thine—and Thine alone,
    This we gladly, fully own;
And, in all our works and ways,
Only now would seek Thy praise.

3 Help us to confess Thy name,
    Bear with joy Thy cross and shame;
Only seek to follow Thee,
Though reproach our portion be.

4 When Thou shalt in glory come,
  And we reach our heav'nly home;
  Louder still each lip shall own,
  We are Thine, and Thine alone.

CCII.—8, 6.

1 WELL may we sing! with triumph sing
    The great Redeemer's praise!
  The glories of the living God,
    Reveal'd in Jesu's face.

2 The Father's love it was, that sought
    From Hell to set us free;
  That gave the Lamb, whose precious blood
    Has seal'd our liberty.

3 In Him we read the Father's love,
    And find eternal peace;
  We meet our God in Jesus Christ,
    And fear and terror cease.

4 Then gladly sing, and sound abroad
    The great Redeemer's praise;
  The glories of the living God,
    The riches of His grace!

CCIII.—8s.

1 God, in the face of His dear Son,
  Makes His eternal counsels known,
  There love in all its glory shines,
  And truth is drawn in fairest lines.

2 The pris'ner there may break his chains,
  The weary rest from all his pains ;
  The captive feel his bondage cease,
  The mourner find the way of peace.

3 There faith reveals to mortal eyes
  A brighter world beyond the skies ;
  There shines the light which guides our way
  From earth to realms of endless day.

4 May we find grace to know the Lord,
  To seek His glories in the word ;
  Its truths with meekness to receive,
  And by its holy precepts live.

CCIV.—8, 6.

1 Come, ye that know the Saviour's name,
    And raise your thoughts above ;

205

Let ev'ry heart and voice unite
To sing—that God is love.

2 This precious truth His word reveals;
And all His mercies prove—
Creation and redemption join
To shew—that God is love.

3 His patience, bearing much and long,
With those who from Him rove,
His kindness when He leads them home,
Both mark—that God is love.

4 The work begun is carried on
By pow'r from heav'n above;
And ev'ry step, from first to last,
Declares—that God is love.

5 O! may we all, while here below,
This best of blessings prove,
Till nobler songs in brighter worlds
Proclaim—that God is love!

CCV.—7s.

1 Songs of praise the angels sang,
Heav'n with hallelujahs rang,

205

When Jehovah's work begun,
When He spake, and it was done.

2 Songs of praise awoke the morn,
When the Prince of Peace was born ·
Songs of praise arose, when He
Captive led captivity.

3 Heav'n and earth must pass away,
Songs of praise shall crown the day :
God will make new heav'ns and earth,
Songs of praise shall hail their birth.

4 And must man alone be dumb,
Till that glorious kingdom come ?
No ;—the church is call'd to raise
Psalms, and hymns, and songs of praise.

5 Let the church then spend her breath,
Singing of the Saviour's death ;
And no less, with heart and voice,
In the Lamb's new life rejoice.

6 Learning thus by faith and love,
Songs of praise to sing above ;
Soon this holy sweet employ
She in glory shall enjoy.

CCVI.—8, 6.

1 I'M not asham'd to own my Lord,
   Or to defend His cause ;
Maintain the honour of His word,
   The glory of His cross.

2 Jesus, my God! I know His name,
   His name is all my trust;
He will not put my soul to shame,
   Nor let my hope be lost.

3 Firm as His life His promise stands,
   And He can well secure
 What I've committed to His hands,
   'Till the appointed hour.

4 Then will He own my worthless name
   Before the Father's face,
And in the new Jerusalem
   Give to my soul its place.

CCVII.—8, 7.

1 FAR from us be grief and sadness,
   Farther still unhallow'd mirth ;
Sons of God may sing with gladness,
   Theirs are joys of heav'nly birth:

Jesus owns them,
He is Lord of heaven and earth.

2 All the worldling's mirth is madness,
    All his labour fruitless toil;
'Tis the saints that taste of gladness,
    Tho' the world their choice revile:
      Sweet their portion,
    Life is in the Saviour's smile.

3 Once the world was all our treasure,
    Then the world our hearts possest;
Now we taste sublimer pleasure,
    Since the Lord has made us blest:
      We can witness,
    Jesus gives His people rest.

CCVIII.—8s.

1 How great the privilege! how sweet,
    To sing of Christ, the Lord we own;
Who gives us hope that we shall sit
    Ere long with Him upon His throne.

2 Is any subject half so sweet,
    So various as the love of God?
Is any other name so great,
    As His Who bore our heavy load?

o

3 'Tis this alone that suits lost man,
   That makes his opposition cease,
Beholding love's amazing plan,
   He drops his arms and sues for peace.

4 'Twas so with us; we once were foes,
   Were foes to Him Who gave us breath:
But He, Whose mercy freely flows
   Has sav'd us from eternal death.

5 Of Him then let us speak and sing,
   Who soon in glory shall appear,
And us in all that glory bring
   His own peculiar throne to share.

CCIX.—8, 6.

1 THOU precious Saviour, Son of God,
   Fountain for guilt and sin,
Sufficient ever is Thy blood
   To cleanse and keep us clean.

2 To us then still that blood apply,
   Till faith to sight improve;
Till hope in full enjoyment die,
   And all our souls are love.

CCX.—8s.

1 ZION shall soon lift up her head,
  And, call'd by grace, arise at length;
From dust, and darkness, and the dead,
  Zion shall rise in Jesus' strength—

2 Shall put her beauteous garments on,
  Salvation, praise, and righteousness:
And, through the world her glory known,
  The heathen shall her God confess.

3 An earthly sun no more her light;
  The clouded moon conceals her face:
Jehovah sheds His glory bright
  On all her scorn'd and sinning race.

4 Then shall her gates wide open stand,
  And she the hallow'd court prepare;
For Gentile hosts in Judah's land
  Shall swell her praise and join her pray'r.

CCXI.—8, 7.

1 THOUGH we're weary, heavy-laden,
  Lost and ruin'd in the fall;

211

God in Christ is our salvation,
He to us is all in all:
Not the righteous,
Sinners Jesus came to call.

2 And for us, though poor and wretched,
(God's redeeming love adore!)
Jesus stands in heav'n a Saviour,
Full of mercy join'd with pow'r;
He is able,
He is willing evermore.

3 Conscience could not make us linger,
Nor of fitness could we dream;
All the fitness He requireth,
Is that we have need of Him:
Jesus gave us
Free salvation in His name.

4 See the Saviour high ascended,
Pleads for us His precious blood;
On the Father's grace depending,
We, thro' Him, the sons of God,
Trust in Jesus,
Who alone the winepress trod.

CCXII.—7s.

1 GLORY to the Father give,
God in Whom we move and live;
Children's praise He loves to hear,
. Children's songs delight His ear.

2 Glory to the First-born bring,
Christ the Prophet, Priest, and King;
Brethren, raise your sweetest strain
To the Lamb Who once was slain!

3 Glory in the Holy Ghost,
Sent from heav'n at Pentecost;
'Tis thro' Him alone we live,
And the precious truth receive.

4 May this then our service be,
Glorying in the Trinity,
For the Gospel from above,
For the word that " God is love."

CCXIII.—8, 6.

1 HAIL ! Alpha and Omega, hail!
The First and Last to faith;
Securer of the Church's hope,
The Truth, the Life, the Path.

2 Hail! First and Last, the great I AM,
    God of the world above!
Increase each little spark of faith,
    Fill ev'ry saint with love.

3 O let that faith which Thou hast taught,
    Be treasur'd in each breast;
The evidence of joys unseen,
    The substance of our rest.

4 Thus shall we go from strength to strength,
    From grace to greater grace;
From each degree of faith move on,
    Till we behold Thy face.

CCXIV.—8s.

1 O RENDER thanks to God above,
The fountain of eternal love;
Whose mercy firm through ages past
Hath stood, and shall for ever last.

2 The Father's changeless love we sing,
Blest fountain! whence our comforts spring:
How great the depth, how high it flows,
No saint can tell, no angel knows.

3 Its length and breadth no eye can trace,
　No thought explore the bounds of grace;
　The love which sav'd our souls from hell,
　Transcends a seraph's tongue to tell.

CCXV.—8, 6.

1 How precious is the book Divine,
　　By inspiration giv'n !
　As a bright lamp its doctrines shine,
　　To guide our souls to heav'n.

2 It sweetly cheers our drooping hearts
　　In this dark vale of tears ;
　Life, light, and joy it still imparts,
　　And quells our rising fears.

3 This lamp, thro' all the tedious night
　　Of life, shall guide our way ;
　'Till we behold the clearer light
　　Of an eternal day.

CCXVI.—8, 6.

1 Now, Lord, inspire each brother's heart,
　　And teach his tongue to speak :
　Food to each hungring soul impart,
　　And cordials to the weak.

2 Yea, God of might, Thy Son reveal,
  And sovereign calling own,
Where Thou hast deign'd to set Thy seal,
  There make His glories known.

3 And let Thy Spirit from above
  Teach us to love Thee more;
Teach us Thy word, that we may love,
  As we did not before.

4 Furnish us all with light and pow'rs
  To walk in wisdom's ways;
So shall the benefit be ours,
  And Thine shall be the praise.

CCXVII.—8, 7, 8, 7, 7, 7.

1 LET us *love*, and *sing*, and *wonder*—
  Let us praise the Saviour's name;
He has hush'd the law's loud thunder,
  He has quench'd mount Sinai's flame;
He has wash'd us in His blood,
He has brought us nigh to God.

2 Let us *love* the Lord that bought us,
  Pity'd us when enemies;.

Called us by His grace, and taught us,
  Gave us ears, and gave us eyes;
He has wash'd us in His blood,
He presents our souls to God.

3 Let us *sing*, though fierce temptation
  Threaten hard to bear us down;
For the Lord, our strong salvation,
  Holds in view the conqu'ror's crown;
He Who wash'd us in His blood,
Safe will bring us home to God.

4 Let us *wonder;* grace and justice
  Join, and point to mercy's store;
Christ hath died; in Him our trust is ;
  Justice smiles, and asks no more;
He Who wash'd us in His blood,
Has secur'd our way to God.

CCXVIII.—Second Part.

1 Let us praise and join the chorus
  Of the Heav'nly Host on high,
Blest ensamples set before us,
  How their praises fill the sky !
Thou hast wash'd us with Thy blood,
Thou art worthy, Lamb of God.

2 Hark! the name of Jesus sounded
  Loud from golden harps above!
Lord, we blush and are confounded,
  Faint our praises, cold our love.
Wash our souls and songs with blood,
For by Thee we come to God.

CCXIX.—8, 8, 6.

1 JOIN'D in the bonds of faith and love,
  With saints on earth and saints above,
    One Spirit with the Lord;
In happy union here we meet,
To worship at the Saviour's feet,
    And own His work and word.

2 Thy gracious presence, Lord, impart;
Display Thy pow'r in ev'ry heart,
    And shed Thy blessing round:
O may Thy truth our spirits cheer,
Confirm our hope, dispel our fear,
    And make our joys abound.

CCXX.—8s.

1 WHAT though the Lord Himself appear
And the last trumpet speak Him near—
The lightnings flash, and thunders roll?
He's welcome to the faithful soul!

2 From heaven let angels' voices sound,—
"See the Almighty Jesus crown'd!"
The saints, sustained by power and grace,
Shall meet the Saviour face to face.

3 Descending thus to take His throne,
To claim the kingdom for His own:
Jesus shall then His bride obtain,
And she with Him for ever reign.

CCXXI.—7s.

1 CHRIST, the Lord, will come again,
None shall wait for Him in vain;
I shall then His glory see:
Christ will come and call for me.

2 Then, when the Archangel's voice
Shakes the earth, and rends the skies,
Rising millions shall proclaim
Blessings on the Saviour's name.

3 "This is our redeeming God!"
Ransom'd hosts will shout aloud:
"Praise, eternal praise be giv'n,
To the Lord of earth and heav'n!"

CCXXII.—8s.

1 JESUS shall reign, where'er the sun
  Doth his successive journies run,
  His kingdom stretch from shore to shore
  'Till moons shall wax and wane no more.

2 People and realms of every tongue,
  Dwell on His love with sweetest song;
  And infant voices shall proclaim
  Their early blessings on His name.

3 Blessings abound, where'er He reigns,
  The pris'ners leap to loose their chains;
  The weary find eternal rest,
  And all the sons of want be blest.

4 Where He displays His healing pow'r,
  Death and the curse shall reign no more;
  But Adam's race in Him shall boast
  More blessings far than Adam lost.

5 Then all the earth shall rise, and bring
  Peculiar honours to its King;
  Angels respond with songs again,
  And earth repeat the loud Amen. .

CCXXIII.—8, 6.

1 BEHOLD! the mountain of the Lord
   In latter days shall rise,
  On mountain tops above the hills,
   And draw the wond'ring eyes.

2 To this the joyful nations round,
   All tribes and tongues, shall flow;
  "Up to the hill of God," say they,
   "And to His house we'll go."

3 The beam that shines from Sion's hill,
   Shall lighten ev'ry land;
  The King who reigns in Salem's tow'rs
   Shall all the world command.

4 Among the nations He shall judge;
   His judgments truth shall guide:
  His sceptre shall protect the just,
   And quell the sinner's pride.

5 No strife shall rage, nor hostile feuds
   Disturb those peaceful years;
  To plough-shares men shall beat their swords,
   To pruning-hooks their spears.

6 No longer hosts encount'ring hosts,
  Shall crowds of slain deplore ;
They hang the trumpet in the hall,
  And study war no more :—

7 For now, O Israel, thou art call'd
  To worship at His shrine ;
And, walking in the light of God,
  In all His grace to shine.

CCXXIV.—8, 8, 6. bis.

1 To wait for that important day,
  When Jesus will His power display;
    Be this our one great care,
  To do His will, our business here ;
  No toil to shun, no danger fear,
    Resolv'd His cross to share.

2 And though He should prolong His stay,
  And sinners mock at the delay,
    His people need not fear;
  The man Who wore the crown of thorns,
  Whose claim the world rejects and scorns,
    In glory will appear.

3 Bright angels shall attend their King,
  And heav'n with acclamations ring,
    When Jesus comes with clouds;
  By faith we see the dazzling train;
  It seems to fill yon azure plain
    With heav'n's exulting crowds.

4 In patience then we now may rest,
  (Assur'd the Father's time is best,)
    And all His word obey:
  For this we know, the day will come
  When Jesus shall convey us home,
    And all His pow'r display.

CCXXV.—8, 6.

1 Lo! what a glorious sight appears
    To our admiring eyes;
  The former seas have pass'd away,
    The former earth and skies.

2 From heav'n the new Jerus'lem comes,
    Full worthy of its Lord;
  See all things now at last renew'd,
    And Paradise restor'd.

3 The God of glory down to men
   Removes His bless'd abode.
He dwells with men, His people they,
  ~ And He His people's God.

4 His gracious hand shall wipe the tears
   From ev'ry weeping eye;
And pains, and groans, and griefs, and fears,
   And death itself shall die.

5 How long, dear Saviour, O how long
   Shall this bright hour delay?
Fly swifter round, ye wheels of time,
   And bring the welcome day.

CCXXVI.—8s.

1 SWEET to the saints it is to bring
Praise to Thy name, O God, and sing;
To show Thy love by morning light,
And tell of all Thy truth by night.

2 For they must triumph in Thee, Lord,
And bless Thy works, and bless Thy word:
To them Thy works so brightly shine!
So deep Thy counsels! so divine!

3 But if the little they can know
  Of Thee and Thine while here below,
  Such triumph gives—what will it be
  When face to face Thyself they see?

CCXXVII.—8s.

1 Jesus, our Lord, our souls adore
  Thy saving love, Thy saving power;
  And, to our utmost stretch of thought,
  Hail the redemption Thou hast wrought.

2 Perish each thought of human pride;
  Let God alone be magnified;
  His glory let the heav'ns resound,
  Shouted from earth's remotest bound!

3 Saints, who above the glory know!
  And ye who taste His love below!
  And every angel join to raise
  Harmonious and eternal praise.

CCXXVIII.—8, 6.

1 Let saints on earth their anthems raise,
  Who taste the Saviour's grace;

P

While they in heav'n proclaim His praise,
And own Him "Prince of Peace."

2 Praise Him Who laid His glory by,
　For man's apostate race;
Praise Him Who stoop'd to bleed and die,
　And own Him "Prince of Peace."

3 We soon shall reach the blissful shore,
　And view His lovely face;
His name for ever to adore,
　And own Him "Prince of Peace."

CCXXIX.—8, 6.

1 COME, saints, and sing; dismiss your fear,
　And raise each drooping head;
Come sing with all the ransom'd here
　The Lamb that once was dead;
Salvation sing: no word more meet
　To join to Jesus' name!
Let ev'ry thankful tongue repeat
　Salvation to the Lamb!

2 When we incurr'd the wrath of God,
　(Alas, what could we worse!)
He came, and with His own life's blood,
　Redeem'd us from the curse:

Salvation sing; no word more meet
  To join to Jesus' name!
Repeat, ye ransom'd souls, repeat
  Salvation to the Lamb!

CCXXX.—8, 6.

1 Or all the gifts Thy hand bestows,
    Thou Giver of all good!
  Not heaven itself a richer knows
    Than the Redeemer's blood.

2 Faith, too, the blood-receiving grace,
    From the same hand we gain;
  Else, sweetly as it suits our case,
    The gift had been in vain.

3 We praise Thee, and would praise Thee more,
    To Thee our all we owe;
  The precious Saviour, and the power
    That makes Him precious too.

CCXXXI.—6, 6, 8, 6.

1 The God of Abr'ham praise,
    Who reigns supreme above!
  Ancient of everlasting days,
    The God of sov'reign love.

2 Jehovah, great I AM—
The Lord our righteousness ;
We hail the blest triumphant name
Our hope of endless bliss.

3 To Thee our songs we raise,
While in this weary land ;
And sing, while waiting for the joys
Which are at Thy right hand.

4 Thou by Thyself hast sworn ;
We on Thine oath depend,
That we ere long, by pow'r upborne,
Shall to the throne ascend,

5 There, to behold Thy face,
There, Thy vast love explore ;
And sing the wonders of Thy grace
A sea without a shore.

CCXXXII.—8, 6.

1 ARM of the Lord, Whose wondrous pow'r
The world and all things made,
Thou art our Rock, and Shield, and Tow'r ;
Our ransom Thou hast paid.

2 Lawgiver, Prophet, Priest, and King,
   The great Deliv'rer Thou;
O may we love Thy praise to sing,
   And feel Thy presence now.

3 Revealer of the Father's love,
   His glory and His pow'r;
Upholding all things now above,
   'Till the appointed hour—

4 Then when Thy foes are all subdued,
   And all Thy work complete,
Thy praise shall be Thy people's food,
   Who in Thy presence wait.

CCXXXIII.—8, 6.

1 Thou great Redeemer, precious Lamb!
   We love to sing of Thee;
No music 's like Thy charming name,
   Nor half so sweet can be.

2 O let us ever hear Thy voice
   To us in mercy speak;
And in our Priest will we rejoice
   Thou great Melchisedec!

3 Our Jesus shall be still our theme,
    While in this world we stay;
  We'll sing our Jesus' blessed name,
    When all things else decay.

4 When we appear upon the cloud,
    With all the favour'd throng,
  Then will we sing more sweet, more loud,
    And Christ shall be our song.

CCXXXIV.—8s.

1 FORGIVENESS! 'twas a joyful sound
    To us when lost and doom'd to die:
  Publish the bliss the world around;
    And gladly shout it thro' the sky.

2 'Twas the rich gift of love divine;
    'Twas full, effacing ev'ry crime:
  Unbounded shall its glories shine,
    And know no change, by changing time.

3 For this stupendous love of Heav'n,
    What grateful honours shall we show!
  Where much transgression is forgiv'n,
    Let love with equal ardour glow.

4 By this inspir'd, let all our days
 With ev'ry heav'nly grace be crown'd;
Let truth and goodness, pray'r and praise,
 In all abide, in all abound.

CCXXXV.—7s.

1 O WHAT blessings flow from grace,
 Treasur'd up in Christ our Head!
We through faith behold His face,
 Standing in our room and stead.

2 Christ our ransom doth appear,
 In the Father's house above:
And His righteousness we wear,
 Lov'd with everlasting love.

CCXXXVI.—7s.

1 Sons of God, now raise your songs;
Praise to Jesus Christ belongs;
Glory to the Saviour's name;
His the Victor's crown and fame.

2 Sore the strife, but rich the prize;
Precious in the Victor's eyes:

Glorious is the work achieved—
Satan vanquish'd, saints reliev'd.

3 Sing we then the Victor's praise,
  Wondrous in His works and ways;
  Bid Him welcome to the throne,
  He is worthy, He alone.

4 Soon, the crown upon His brow,
  Every knee to Him shall bow;
  While the full creation sings,
  "Lord of lords" and "King of kings!"

CCXXXVII.—8, 6.

1 Behold the glories of the Lamb
    Upon the Father's throne!
  Prepare new honours for His name,
    And songs before unknown.

2 Let elders worship at His feet,
    The church adore around,
  With vials full of odours sweet,
    And harps of sweeter sound.

3 Now to the Lamb that once was slain
    Be endless blessings paid:
Salvation, glory, joy remain,
    For ever on His head!

4 Thou hast redeem'd our souls with blood,
    Hast set the pris'ners free;
Hast made us kings and priests to God,
    And we shall reign with Thee.

CCXXXVIII.—8, 6.

1 In Him Whose presence gladdens heaven,
    We do, and will rejoice;
How blest are they to whom 'tis giv'n,
    To hear and know His voice.

2 He might have left us to endure
    The wrath we seem'd to brave;
Our case would then admit no cure,
    For who but He can save.

3 But though resisted long, He strove;
    His purpose was to save;
He show'd the greatness of His love,
    And though provok'd, forgave.

4 Then let us sing of grace alone,
   And magnify the name
Of Him Who sits upon the throne,
   And join to praise the Lamb.

CCXXXIX.—7s.

1 ENDLESS praises to our Lord,
Ever be His name ador'd !
Angels, own Him, own the Lamb;
He is worthy—praise His name.

2 Saints adore Him, sound His fame,
   You He saved from endless shame;
Saints and angels jointly sing,
   Glory to the Priest and King.

CCXL.—8s.

1 IT was for me the Lord did die,
   To clear me from all charge of sin;
And, Lord, from guilt of crimson dye,
   Thy precious blood hath made me clean.

2 And now Thy righteousness divine
   Is all my glory, all my trust;
Nor will I fear, since that is mine,
   While Thou dost live, and God is just.

3 Clad in this robe how bright I shine!
　　Angels might covet such a dress;
　Angels have not a robe like mine,
　　A robe like Jesus' righteousness.

CCXLI.—7s.

1 HOLY Lamb, who Thee receive,
　Who in Thee begin to live;
　Day and night they cry to Thee,
　"As Thou art, so let us be."

2 Fix, O fix each wavering mind,
　To Thy cross our spirits bind;
　Earthly passions far remove,
　Swallow up our souls in love.

3 Dust and ashes though we be,
　Full of guilt and misery;
　Thine we are, Thou Son of God,
　Take the purchase of Thy blood.

4 Boundless wisdom, power divine,
　Love unspeakable, are Thine;
　Praise by all to Thee be given,
　Sons of God, and hosts of heaven.

CCXLII.—8, 6.

1 O TEACH me more of Thy blest ways,
  Thou Holy Lamb of God!
And fix and root me in Thy grace,
  As one redeem'd by blood.

2 O tell me often of Thy love,
  Of all Thy grief and pain;
And let my heart with joy confess,
  From thence comes all my gain.

3 For this, O may I freely count
  Whate'er I have but loss;
The dearest object of my love,
  Compared with Thee, but dross.

4 Engrave this deeply on my heart
  With an eternal pen,
That I may, in some small degree,
  Return Thy love again.

CCXLIII.—6, 6, 6, 6, 8, 8.

1 GIVE thanks to God most high,
  The Father of our Lord,
The sov'reign King of kings,
  And be His name ador'd.

244

Thy mercy, God, shall still endure,
Thy word abide for ever sure.

2 He sent His only Son
    To save us from our woe ;
From Satan, guilt, and hell,
    And ev'ry hurtful foe.
Thy mercy, Lord, shall still endure,
Thy word abide for ever sure.

3 Give thanks aloud to God,
    To God your praises bring,
With all around His throne
    His works and glories sing.
His pow'r and grace are still the same,
Let endless praise exalt His name.

CCXLIV.—6, 8, 6.

1 THROUGH waves, through clouds and storms
    God gently clears our way ;
We wait His time ; so shall the night
    Soon end in blissful day.

2 He ev'ry where hath sway,
    And all things serve His might ;

His ev'ry act pure blessing is
His path unsullied light.

3 When He makes bare His arm,
   What shall His work withstand?
When He His people's cause defends,
   Who then shall stay His hand?

4 We leave it to Himself,
   To choose and to command,
With wonder fill'd, we soon shall see
   How wise, how strong His hand.

5 We comprehend Him not,
   Yet earth and heaven tell;
God sits as soy'reign on the throne,
   And ruleth all things well.

6 Thou seest our weakness, Lord,
   Our hearts are known to Thee;
O lift Thou up each sinking hand,
   Confirm each feeble knee.

7 And let us henceforth all
   Boldly Thy truth declare,
Confessing unto all we meet
   Thy love and guardian care.

CCXLV.—8, 6.

1 God knew the church—unsought, He sought;
  Wondrous His love has been;
With Jesus' blood He sav'd and bought,
  And freed her from her sin.

2 He keeps her now—securely keeps,
  Whatever foe assails;
With vigilance that never sleeps,
  With pow'r that never fails.

3 He gives her hope that she shall be
  Ere long with Him above;
That she shall all His glory see,
  And celebrate His love.

4 Then let us, while we dwel below
  Obey the Father's voice;
To all His dispensations bow,
  And in His name rejoice.

5 How sweet to hear Him say at last,
  "Ye blessed children, come,
Sorrow and crying now are past,
  And heav'n is now your home."

17-

he holy   people

Redeemed of the

CLXXIV.—6

The day comes on

Soon shall the

Who trust the S

Shall see His fa

The clouds that

Shall quickly al

2   Ye saints lift up

Salvation

See wher

Its nd

let the

The La

...ther's pity dost Thou feel
... all Thy feeble saints;
... the tend'rest accents speak,
... soothe their sad complaints?

... support our souls shall lean,
... banish ev'ry care;
... darkest path is cheer'd with smiles,
... Thou art with us there.

CCXLVIII.—8, 6.

... we are seen, O God, by Thee,
This is our happy thought;
... to Thine eye,
And ... forgot.

... the light
W... our ways;
And ... ight gloom
T... displays.

3 Th... we'll pass;
... die,
Th... will not dread,
... nigh.

CCXLVI.—8s.

1 O God! we see Thee in the Lamb,
  To be our hope, our joy, our rest,
The glories that compose Thy name
  Standing engag'd to make us blest.

2 Thou great and good! Thou just and wise!
  Hail! as our Father and our God!
For we are Thine by sacred ties,
  Thy sons and daughters, bought with blood.

3 Then, ah! to us this grace afford,
  That far from Thee we ne'er may move;
Our guard—the presence of the Lord,
  Our joy—the sense of pardoning love.

4 For this will make our hearts rejoice,
  Turning to light our darkest days;
And this will nerve each feeble voice,
  While we have breath to pray or praise.

CCXLVII.—8, 6.

1 And art Thou with us, gracious Lord,
  To dissipate our fear;
Dost Thou proclaim Thyself *our* God,
  Our Father ever near?

2 A father's pity dost Thou feel
  For all Thy feeble saints;
And in the tend'rest accents speak,
  To soothe their sad complaints?

3 On this support our souls shall lean,
  And banish ev'ry care;
The darkest path is cheer'd with smiles,
  Since Thou art with us there.

CCXLVIII.—8, 6.

1 THAT we are seen, O God, by Thee,
  This is our happy thought;
Presented faultless to Thine eye,
  And all our sins forgot.

2 Each hour of joy, this is the light
  Which guides us in our ways;
And in affliction's midnight gloom
  This truth its pow'r displays.

3 Then boldly on thro' life we'll pass;
  And if we're call'd to die,
The valley's shade we will not dread,
  For Thou wilt still be nigh.

Q

CCXLIX.—8, 6.

1 OUR feeble pray'r we now present
  Before the throne of grace;
God of the fathers! be our guide
  Through all the toilsome race.

2 Through each perplexing path of life
  Our pilgrim footsteps guide;
Save us each day from Satan's wiles,
  And full escape provide.

3 O spread Thine own protection round,
  Till all our wand'rings cease,
And at our Father's lov'd abode
  We all arrive in peace!

4 We ask through Him, by Whose kind hand
  Thine own were ever led;
Who in Thy presence stands confess'd,
  The Church's glorious Head.

CCL.—8, 8, 8, 4.

1 'Tis seldom we can trace the way
  Where Thou, our gracious Lord, dost move;
But we can always surely say,
  'That God is love.

2 When fear its gloomy cloud will fling
   O'er earth—our souls to heav'n above,
As to their sanctuary, spring,
    For God is love.

3 When doubt hangs o'er our darken'd path,
   We'll check our dread, each doubt reprove:
For here Thy church sweet comfort hath,
    That God is love.

4 Yes Thou art love—a truth like this
   Can ev'ry gloomy thought remove,
And turn our tears and woes to bliss;
    Our God is love.

CCLI.—8, 6.

1 THY Brethren, Lord, so minded keep,
   That we know nought beside
Thee, Who wast slain us to redeem,
   Thee! Jesus crucified!

2 O may we, Saviour, step for step,
   Bear Thee sweet company,
So will whate'er we undertake
   An act of worship be!

3 May we to Thee in all our wants,
   Child-like, still closer fly,

Directing still throughout our course,
By faith to Thee the eye!

4 Although but little we can do,
Yet 'tis our heart's desire,
To do whate'er will give Thee joy;
No more do we require.

CCLII.—8s.

1 O Love divine! what hast Thou done?
The Son of God His blood hath shed,
The Father's co-eternal Son
Had all our sins upon Him laid;
The Son of God for us hath died,
Our Lord, our Life was crucified,—

2 Was crucified for us in shame,
To bring us, rebels, back to God;
So we may glory in His name,
For we are cleansed by His blood:
Pardon and life flow'd from His side,
When He, the Lord, was crucified.

3 Then let us glory in the cross,
And make it here our constant theme;
All things for Christ account but dross,
And give up all our hearts to Him.
Of nothing speak or think beside,
The Lord, Who here was crucified.

CCLIII.—6, 6, 8, 6.

1 LIKE sheep we went astray
    Far from the fold of God,
Each wand'ring in a diff'rent way,
    But all the downward road.

2 How dreadful was the hour
    When God our wand'rings laid,
And did at once His vengeance pour,
    Upon the Shepherd's head !

3 How glorious was the grace
    When Jesus suffer'd thus ;
His guiltless life the Shepherd pays,
    To give that life to us !

4 His honour and His breath
    Were taken both away ;
Join'd with the wicked in His death,
    And made as vile as they.

5 Gladly He bow'd His head
    For us, the sons of men,
That we by Him, the woman's seed,
    Might conquer death and pain.

CCLIV.—8s.

1 THE Lamb was slain! let us adore,
   And joyfully His mercy own,
And humbly now and evermore
   Before His wounded feet fall down;
Serve without dread, with rev'rence love
The Lord Whose boundless grace we prove.

2 The Lamb was slain! both day and night
   The angelic choirs His praises sing;
To Him enthron'd above all height,
   They round the throne their anthems bring;
As saints on earth we join the song,
And praise Him tho' with stamm'ring tongue.

3 Gladly our own poor works we leave,
   For Him despise wealth, pleasure, fame,
To Him our souls and bodies give,
   Whose love doth our affections claim;
Henceforth we own Him as our Lord,
Alone belov'd—alone ador'd.

4 Through Him alone we live, for He
   Hath drowned our transgressions all
In love's unfathomable sea:
   O love, unknown, unsearchable!

The holy Lamb for sin was slain,
That sinners endless life might gain.

5 As ground, when parch'd with summer's heat,
 Gladly drinks in the welcome show'r,
So would we, list'ning at His feet,
 Receive His words, and feel His pow'r;
Let nothing in our hearts remain
But this great truth, "The Lamb was slain!"

CCLV.—8, 6.

1 O THOU, Whose mercies far exceed
 All we can do or say,
As in Thy people Thou indeed
 Dost daily more display;
Let, for our happiness, O God,
 On us while here below,
By virtue of Thy death and blood,
 Thy richest blessings flow.

2 Preserve Thy flock most graciously,
 Within Thy shelt'ring fold,
Move them from ev'ry harm away,
 And in Thy safeguard hold;
Till Thou shalt fully have obtain'd
 In us the fruits of grace,
And we, in joys that never end,
 Shall see Thee, face to face.

3 O may the very God of peace,
    Us wholly sanctify,
And grant us such a rich increase
    Of unction from on high ;
That spirit, soul, and body may,
    Preserved free from stain,
Be blameless until Thy great day ;
    Lord Jesus Christ, Amen !

CCLVI.—8, 8, 7, 8, 8, 8, 7.

1 O HOW the thought that I shall know
Jesus that suffer'd here below,
    To manifest God's favour,
For me, and for the saints I love,
Both here, and with Himself above,
Doth my renewed nature move
    At that sweet word, " For ever ! "

2 For ever to behold Him shine !
For evermore to call Him mine !
    And see Him still before me ;
For ever on His face to gaze !
And meet His full assembled rays,
While all the Father He displays
    To all the saints in glory !

3 Not all things else are half so dear
As His delightful presence here,
    What must it be in heaven !

'Tis heav'n on earth that we can say,
As now we journey, day by day,
"Himself has borne our sins away,
   Our sins are all forgiven."

4 But how will His celestial voice
  Make each enraptur'd heart rejoice,
   When we in glory hear Him!
  When we no longer at the gate,
  But in His blessed presence, wait,
  When Jesus on His throne of state
   Invites us to come near Him!

CCLVII.—6, 6, 8, 6.

1 OUR times are in Thy hand,
   Father, we wish them there;
  Our life, our soul, our all, we leave
   Entirely to Thy care.

2 Our times are in Thy hand,
   Whatever they may be,
  Pleasing or painful, dark or bright,
   As best may seem to Thee.

3 Our times are in Thy hand,
   Why should we doubt or fear?
  A Father's hand will never cause
   His child a needless tear.

4 Our times are in Thy hand,
　Jesus the crucified !
　The hand our many sins had pierc'd
　　Is now our guard and guide.

5 Our times are in Thy hand,
　Jesus the Advocate !
　Nor can that hand be stretch'd in vain,
　　For us to supplicate.

6 Our times are in Thy hand ;
　. We 'll always trust in Thee,
　Till we have left this weary land,
　　And all Thy glory see.

CCLVIII.—8s.

1 WHERE high the heav'nly temple stands
The house of God not made with hands,
A great High Priest our nature wears,
And there before our God appears.

2 He Who for us as surety stood,
And pour'd on earth His precious blood,
Pursues in heav'n His gracious plan,
The Saviour and the Friend of man.

3 Though now ascended up on high,
He bends on earth a Brother's eye ;

Partaker of the human name,
He knows the frailty of our frame.

4 Our Fellow-suff'rer still retains,
A fellow-feeling of our pains ;
And still remembers in the skies,
His tears, and grief, and agonies.

5 In ev'ry pang that rends the heart,
The " Man of Sorrows " had a part,
He knows and feels our every grief,
And gives the suff'ring saint relief.

6 With boldness therefore, at the throne,
Let us make all our sorrows known ;
And seek the aid of heav'nly pow'r
To help us in each trying hour.

CCLIX.—8s.

1 HOSANNA ! to the living Lord ;
Hosanna ! to th' incarnate Word ;
To Christ, Creator, Saviour, King,
Let earth, let heav'n, hosanna sing

2 Hosanna ! Lord, Thine angels cry,
Hosanna ! Lord, Thy saints reply ;
Above, beneath us, and around,
We would that all should swell the sound.

3 Assembled in Thy blessed name,
Here we Thy parting promise claim,
Then, Saviour, with protecting care,
Present to God our praise and prayer.

CCLX.—6, 6, 8, 6.

1 To God, the only wise,
    Father, and Son, we sing,
And high enthron'd above the skies,
    Praises to Them we bring.

2 'Tis God's eternal love,
    His counsel and His care,
Preserve us safe from sin and shame,
    And ev'ry hurtful snare.

3 He will present His saints,
    Unblemish'd and complete,
Before the glory of His face,
    With Him enthron'd to sit.

4 Then all His chosen seed
    Shall meet around the throne,
To bless the triumph of His grace,
    And make His glories known.

· 5 To our Redeemer, God,
  Almighty pow'r belongs;
  We soon shall reach His bless'd abode,
  And shout triumphant songs.

CCLXI.—8, 6.

1 To Thee, O gracious Lord, we give
  Our spirit, body, soul;
  Surcharge our hearts with love of Thee,
  And baser loves control.

2 Then will our converse be in heav'n,
  Thy praise our tongues employ;
  We shall forget all else but Thee,
  Our glory, crown, and joy.

3 But oh! our Brother, Husband, Friend,
  We dread the things below,
  Lest they attempt to win our hearts,
  And we our hearts bestow.

4 Thou know'st us, fickle, foolish, frail,
  Inconstant as the air,
  Through Thee alone can we escape
  Temptation's constant snare.

5 Lord we look up, we turn to Thee,
   We seek Thy face above,
Look, Lord, on us, and let us feel
   Th' omnipotence of love.

CCLXII.—8, 8, 6.

1 NOTHING on earth we call our own,
   As strangers to the world, unknown,
      We'd all its joys despise;
   We'd trample on its whole delight,
   And seek a city out of sight,
      A city in the skies.

2 There is our house and portion fair,
   Our treasure and our hearts are there,
      And our abiding home;
   For us our martyr'd brethren stay,
   And angels call us hence away,
      And Jesus bids us come.

3 "We come,"—Thy servants, Lord, reply,
   " We come to meet Thee in the sky,
      And claim our heav'nly rest;
   Soon let our toilsome journey end,
   For then, O Saviour, Brother, Friend,
      With Thee we shall be blest."

CCLXIII.—7, 7, 7, 7, 8, 8.

1 " ONWARD let My children go;"
Jesu's God hath written so;
Though the path be through the sea,
Little flock what's that to thee?
He Who bids thee pass the waters
Will be with His sons and daughters.

2 Deep and wide the sea appears,
Every soul is fill'd with fears—
Yet the word is " Onward" still,—
Forward move to do His will,
Tho' no way thou canst discover,
Not one plank to float thee over.

3 Art thou feeble, sorely tried?
Art thou press'd on every side?
Does it seem as if no pow'r
Could relieve thee in this hour?
Wherefore art thou thus dishearten'd?
Is the arm that sav'd thee, shorten'd?

4 Stand thou still, and thou shalt see
Wonders wrought, and wrought for thee;
Safe thyself, on yonder shore,
Thou shalt see thy foes no more:

Thine to see the Saviour's glory,
Thine to tell a wondrous story.

5   Trust thy God, and He'll be known,
    Far and wide, as God alone;
    At His feet thy fears shall fall,
    For thy God is Lord of all;
    Strength is His, and His salvation,
    Make them both thy sure foundation.

CCLXIV.—8, 6.

1 BELOV'D associates in the strife
    That ends in perfect peace,
A life of conflict is our life,
    From war we must not cease.

2 The soldiers of the cross must fight,
    Till life itself be past;
The foe assails them day and night,
    Assails them to the last.

3 But let us still remember this,
    Though mighty are our foes,
The Lord Who saves us, greater is
    Than all who can oppose.

4 We need not fly, we need not fear,
    Since He Who reigns above,

In all our conflicts will be near
The people of His love.

5 If thus we face the adverse pow'rs,
  If thus we meet the strife,
The vict'ry always must be ours,
  And ours the crown of life.

CCLXV.—8s.

1 AND do we hope to be with Him,
  Who on the cross resign'd His breath,
Who died a victim to redeem
  His people from eternal death?

2 Then should the question oft recur,
  What do we more than others do?
How do we show that we prefer
  The things above to things below?

3 Where is the holy walk that suits
  The name and character we bear?
And where are seen those heav'nly fruits
  That show we're not what once we were?

4 Allied to Him Who bore the cross,
  And call'd the people of the Lord,
The world to us should seem but loss,
  And worthless all it can afford.

R

5 As pilgrims on their journey home,
   'Tis thus His people should be found,
Who seek a city yet to come,
   And cannot rest on earthly ground.

6 'Tis thus His people prove their birth,
   'Tis thus they glorify their Lord;
To others they resign the earth,
   And hasten to their bright reward.

CCLXVI.—6s

1 If Jesus should appear
   Now at this very moment,
 We have no cause to fear;
   No, but with deep abasement,
Joyful we would adore
   The Lamb Who shed His blood,
And own Him evermore
   Our Saviour, Lord and God.

2 Ah! might the time soon come,
   When Thou, our souls' Belov'd,
Shalt take Thy brethren home,
   And shew them all approv'd;
When we shall all behold
   Him Whom by faith we know,
Chief Shepherd of the fold,
   Saviour from ev'ry foe!

3 Hear Thou. Thy people's cry,
　O Jesus, Christ and Lord,
And bring that glory nigh
　As promis'd in Thy word;
And when Thou shalt assign
　His lot to ev'ry one,
Thy righteousness divine
　Shall be our boast alone.

CCLXVII.—6, 6, 8, 6.

1 Ye servants of the Lord!
　Each in his office wait,
Observant of His heavenly word,
　And watchful at His gate

2 Let ev'ry lamp be bright,
　And trim each golden flame,
Gird up your loins, as in His sight,
　And called by His name.

3 Watch! 'tis your Lord's command,
　And while we speak He's near,
Mark the first signal of His hand,
　And ready all appear.

4 O happy servant he,
　In such a posture found,
He shall his Lord with rapture see,
　And be with honour crown'd.

5 Christ shall the banquet spread
   With His own bounteous hand,
And raise that fav'rite servant's head
   Amid the happy band.

CCLXVIII.—7s.

1 Son of God, Thy people's shield,
   Must we still Thine absence mourn ?
Let Thy promise be fulfill'd,—
   Thou hast said " I will return."

2 Gracious Master, soon appear,
   Quickly bring Thy morning's light,
Then will cease the constant tear,
   Hope be turn'd to joyful sight.

3 As a woman counts the days
   Till her absent lord she see,
Longs and watches, weeps and prays,
   So the church must long for Thee.

4 Come, that we may see Thee nigh;
   Then the sheep shall feed in peace,
Hush'd for ever trouble's sigh,
   Sin and sorrow's triumph cease.

CCLXIX.—8, 6.

1 Long hath the night of sorrow reign'd,
   The dawn will bring us light;
Christ shall appear, and we shall rise
   With gladness at the sight.

2 Then we shall see the blessed Lamb,
   Shall see Him and rejoice;
His coming like the morning be,
   Like morning songs His voice.

3 As dew upon the tender herb,
   Diffusing fragrance round,
As show'rs that usher in the spring,
   And cheer the thirsty ground;

4 So shall His gracious presence bless,
   And give us joyful light;
That hallow'd morn will chase away
   All sorrows of the night.

CCLXX.—8s.

1 O Saviour! Whom absent we love;
   Whom not having seen we adore,
Whose name is exalted above
   All glory, dominion, and pow'r.

2 When that happy morning begins,
   When we in Thy glories shall shine,
Nor grieve any more by our sins
   The bosom on which we recline;

3 O then shall the mists be remov'd,
   And round us Thy brightness be pour'd!
We shall meet Him, Whom absent we lov'd,
   We shall see, Whom unseen we ador'd.

4 And then never more shall the fears,
   The trials, temptations, and woes,
Which darken this valley of tears,
   Intrude on our blissful repose.

CCLXXI.—8s.

1 BEHOLD the saints belov'd of God,
   Who wash'd their robes in Jesu's blood;
More spotless than the purest white,
   They shine in uncreated light.

2 From tribulation great they came,
   They bore the cross and scorn'd the shame;
But now in joy unceasing rest,
   With God in glory fully blest.

3 The cross has prov'd their endless gain ;
  With Jesus they'll for ever reign ;
  And seated on His throne, shall praise
  The blessings of redeeming grace.

4 Hunger they ne'er shall feel again,
  Nor burning thirst shall they sustain ;
  To wells of living water led,
  By God the Lamb for ever fed.

5 Jesus, the Saviour, is their theme ;
  They sing the wonders of His name ;
  To Him ascribing pow'r and grace,
  Dominion and eternal praise.

6 " Amen !" they cry to Him alone,
  Once dead, now seated on His throne ;
  To Him be glory, and again
  To Him be praise, " Amen ! Amen !"

CCLXXII.—8, 6.

1 How bright these glorious spirits shine,
  Whence all their bright array !
  How came they to the happy seats
  Of everlasting day ?

2 Lo! these are they from suff'rings great,
   Who came to realms of light,
And in the blood of Christ have wash'd
   Their robes, which shine so bright.

3 Now with triumphant palms they stand
   Before the throne on high;
And serve the Lord they love, amidst
   The glories of the sky.

4 His presence fills each heart with joy,
   And gives them pow'r to sing;
While day, and night, the sacred courts
   With glad hosannas ring.

5 Hunger and thirst are felt no more,
   Nor sun with scorching ray;
God is their sun, whose cheering beams
   Give them eternal day.

6 The Lamb, Who dwells amid the throne,
   Shall o'er them still preside,
Feed them with nourishment divine,
   And all their footsteps guide.

7 Midst pastures green He'll lead His flock,
   Where living streams appear,
And God the Lord, from ev'ry eye
   Shall wipe off ev'ry tear.

CCLXXIII.—8, 6.

1 Now may the God of peace and love,
    Who, from the silent grave,
Restor'd the Shepherd of the sheep,
    Omnipotent to save,—

2 Through the rich merits of that blood
    Which He on Calv'ry spilt,
To make the gracious work secure,
    On which our hopes are built,—

3 Perfect our souls in ev'ry grace,
    To do His blessed will,
And all that's pleasing in His sight
    Inspire us to fulfil.

4 For Him, our ris'n Shepherd's sake,
    We ev'ry blessing pray;
With glory let His name be crown'd
    Through heav'n's eternal day.

CCLXXIV.—8s.

Saviour and Lord, our Priest and King,
    Who didst for our transgressions die,
Bearing our grief, that Thou might'st bring
    Pardon and immortality;

Grant to our voice a seraph's wing
  To bear Thy praises up on high,
Dominion, blessing, might, we'll sing
  To Thee, throughout eternity;
Amen ! Amen ! Our God, Amen.

CCLXXV.—8s.

1 THE Lord is coming in the clouds,
  Is coming with angelic crowds,
  An universal shout shall rend
  The air, and Jesus will descend.

2 How grand the pomp of His descent,
  What glory waits on the event !
  The glory that to heav'n belongs,
  Is His, and His the angels' songs.

3 Unlike to those who nothing see
  Beyond the world, those men should be,
  Who look for Jesus in the air,
  And know that they shall meet Him there.

4 Their girded loins, and lamps of fire
  Should tell what is their souls' desire,
  To see the object of their love,
  And dwell with Him in heav'n above.

CCLXXVI.—8, 8, 6.

1 JEHOVAH, Jesus! glorious Lord,
We seek Thy Spirit with the word,
　　For all Thy saints around:
We seek for each of Thine now here,
The seeing eye, the hearing ear,
　　To know the joyful sound!

2 Without a flowing stream of grace,
To see God's glory in Thy face,
　　And manifest *Thee*, Lord;
Our meetings here must barren prove
Not one can taste the Father's love,
　　Or savour of the word.

3 The Holy Ghost, in blessing thus,
Must take of Thine and shew to us,
　　Thine own and God's impart;
And He no less the same must prove,
And shed abroad the Father's love,
　　In each renewed heart;

4 Yet Lord! Thy grace we dare not bound·
Near to Thyself we've always found
　　The Holy Ghost is ours:
Thy Person is the blessed clue
To all who would the Father view
　　And know the Spirit's powers.

CCLXXVII.—SECOND PART.

1 SHEPHERD of life ! do Thou behold
  The little ones within the fold,
      With special grace, this day;
  That all God's children giv'n to Thee,
  May have their portion full and free,
      And none go lean away.

2 That fully taught, we all may boast
  In Father, Son, and Holy Ghost;
      For this to us is giv'n;
  That each may say, in godly fear,
  " Rejoice, ye saints, the Lord is near,
      He 'll quickly come from heav'n."

CCLXXVIII.—8s.

1 How precious that truth to the soul,
    " That Christ and His people are one ;"
  He life-giving Head to the whole,
    They members, and bone of His bone.

2 An union so firm and so sure,
    Will bear the severest review,
  In Jesus the whole is secure,
    And nothing its bands can undo.

3 This union assures us of bliss,
  Secur'd in the Head of all pow'rs ;
We've portion in all that is His,
  And Jesus in all that is ours.

4 Hence the church, tho' by nature so mean
  (In itself it is nothing but sin),
In Jesus is perfectly clean,
  And holy and righteous in Him.

CCLXXIX.—SECOND PART.

1 How wond'rous the glories that meet
  In Jesus, and from His face shine !
His love is eternal and sweet,
  'Tis human, 'tis also divine !

2 His glory—not only God's Son—
  In manhood He had His full part,—
And the union of both joined in one,
  Form the fountain of love in His heart.

3 Ye wash'd in the blood of the Lamb,
  Remember, when sorrows press sore,
Your Jesus did once feel the same,
  When conflicts and trials He bore.

4 Your Jesus both knows and hath felt,
   What marks all our sorrows and fears,
Since here in the flesh He once dwelt,
   And offer'd strong crying and tears.

5 And we, as redeemed, well know,
   This Jesus the same in His love;
The feet cannot suffer below,
   And the Head be unconscious above!

6 And all that He has, He will use,
   For the Church 'mid her sorrows and woes,
While the truth of His God she pursues,
   Nor aught of His conflict foregoes.

7 The merits and worth of His blood,
   Have rais'd us from hell and from fear,
That we as the blest sons of God,
   Might make His good pleasure our care

8 O then may this union and love
   Make us walk in the service of Heaven,
Mid' obedience and suff'ring to prove
   That we to the Lamb had been giv'n.

CCLXXX.—8, 6.

1 WORTHY the Lamb for sinners slain
   (Cry the redeem'd above),

Blessing and honour to obtain,
And everlasting love.

2 Hail! Hallelujah! power and praise
To God in Christ be given!
May all who now this anthem raise
Renew the strain in heaven!

CCLXXXI.—8, 6.

1 JESUS, Thou source of true delight,
Whom we unseen adore,
Unveil our souls to all Thy light,
That we may love Thee more,

2 Thy glory o'er creation shines;
But in the sacred Word
We read in fairer, brighter lines,
The glories of our Lord.

3 'Tis here, whene'er our comforts droop,
And sins and sorrows rise,
Thy love with cheerful beams of hope
Each fainting heart supplies.

4 Jesus, our Lord, our Life, our Light,
O come with blissful ray:
Break through the gloomy shades of night,
And bring the look'd for day.

5 Then shall each soul with rapture trace
  The wonders of Thy love ;
And the full glories of Thy face,
  As known to those above.

CCLXXXII.—8, 7.

1 WHY those fears ? behold 'tis Jesus
  Holds the helm, and guides the ship ;
Spread the sails, and catch the breezes
  Sent to waft us through the deep,
    To the regions
  Where the mourners cease to weep.

2 Could we stay where death is hovering ?
  Could we rest on such a shore ?
No ; the awful truth discovering,
  We could linger there no more ;
    We forsake it,
  Leaving all we lov'd before.

3 Though the shore we hope to land on,
  Only by report is known,
Yet we freely all abandon,
  Led by that report alone,
    And with Jesus,
  Through the trackless deep move on.

4 Led by that, we brave the ocean;
    Led by that, the storm defy;
Calm amidst tumultuous motion,
    Knowing that our Lord is nigh:
        Waves obey Him,
    And the storms before Him fly.

5 Render'd safe by His protection,
    We shall pass the wat'ry waste
Trusting to His wise direction,
    We shall gain the port at last;
        And with wonder,
    Think on toils and dangers past.

6 O what pleasures there await us!
    There the tempests cease to roar:
There it is that those who hate us
    Can molest our peace no more:
        Trouble ceases
    On that tranquil, happy shore.

CCLXXXIII.—8, 8, 6.

1 To those who love Thee, gracious Lord,
How bright, how precious is the Word,
    By God in mercy given,

s

A guide to all who, travelling here
Mid sin and darkness, death and fear,
   Are pressing on to heaven.

2 O gracious Saviour, God of love,
  Aid Thine own Spirit from above,
    And fill us with desire
To read, to mark, to learn Thy will,
And with Thy truth our spirits fill,
    And touch our hearts with fire.

3 And till in glory Thou dost come
  To take Thy waiting people home,
    With those at Thy right hand ;
E'en till that great and dreadful day,
When heaven and earth shall pass away,
    May we in service stand !

CCLXXXIV.—8, 6.

1 Look, look, ye Saints, within the veil ;
   To Jesus raise your song,
Your joys can never, never fail,
   For you to Him belong.

2 O happy saints, for ever freed
   From guilt, and every care ;

Dwell, dwell with your exalted Head,
  And let your life be there.

3 And glory in your conq'ring God;
  See, see Him as He is;
  Your robes are spotless through His blood,
  Your happiness is His.

4 O think not of this world of woe,
  Though subject still to grief;
  But seek your portion there to know,
  For this will give relief.

5 Aye trust, for ever trust in God,
  For ev'ry promise giv'n;
  And dwell with Him through Jesu's blood,
  Within the veil of heav'n.

CCLXXXV.—8s.

1 THOU hidden love of God, Whose height,
  Whose depth unfathom'd no man knows,
I see from far Thy beauteous light,
  And gladly seek in it repose;
That thus my heart from earth set free,
May find its whole delight in Thee!

2 O crucify this self, that I
   No more, but Christ in me may live;
And bid each vile affection die,
   Nor let one hateful lust survive;
In all things nothing may I see,
Nothing desire, or seek, but Thee.

CCLXXXVI.—8s.

1 Jesus, Thy boundless love to me
   No thought can reach, no tongue declare;
Then bend my wayward heart to Thee,
   And reign without a rival there:
Thine, wholly Thine, alone I'd live;
Myself to Thee entirely give.

2 O Lord, how cheering is Thy way!
   How blest! how gracious in mine eyes!
Care, anguish, sorrow, pass away,
   And fear before Thy presence flies
O Jesus, nothing may I see,
Nothing desire, or seek but Thee!

3 'Mid conflict be Thy love my peace!
   In weakness be Thy love my strength!

And when the storms of life shall cease,
  And Thou to earth shalt come at length,
Then to Thy glory be my Guide,
And show me Him Who for me died.

CCLXXXVII.—6, 6, 8, 6.

1 Ye saints, attend the cry!
    Attend the trumpet's sound:
  Stand to your arms, the foe is nigh,
    And pow'rs of hell are round.

2 Consider Christ, your Head—
    Your Captain's footsteps see;
  Follow the Saviour, and be led
    To certain victory.

3 All pow'r to Him is giv'n—
    He ever reigns the same;
  Salvation, happiness, and heav'n,
    Are yours in Jesu's name.

4 Our Captain leads us on;
    He beckons from the skies;
  He reaches out the starry crown,
    And bids us take the prize.

5 We bow to His command,
　Our arms and hearts prepare ;
And firmly in the battle stand,
　To wage a glorious war.

CCLXXXVIII.—6, 6, 8, 6.

1 Thou very present aid,
　In suff'ring and distress,
The soul, which still on Thee is staid,
　Is kept in perfect peace.

2 Calmly the heart reclin'd
　By faith on Jesu's breast—
In deepest woe exults to find
　A sweet eternal rest.

3 Jesus, to Whom we fly,
　Does all our wishes fill,
In vain the creature-streams are dry,
　We have a Fountain still.

4 Bereav'd of earthly friends,
　We find them all in One !
And peace, and joy, that never ends
　And heaven—in Christ alone !

CCLXXXIX.—6, 6, 8, 6.

1 FROM earth the Saviour's gone,
   And stands before our God;
   And sprinkled now is all the throne,
   With His atoning blood.

2 No fiery vengeance now,
   No burning wrath comes down,
   Where Justice calls for sinners' blood,
   The Saviour shews His own.

3 Then may our joyful tongues
   Our Maker's praises sing;
   Jesus, the Priest, receives our songs,
   And bears them to the King.

4 We bow before His face,
   And sound His glories high;
   "Hosanna to the God of grace,
   That brought the guilty nigh."

CCXC.—8, 6.

1 Joy to the world! the Lord is come!
   Let earth receive her King;
   Let every heart prepare Him room,
   And all creation sing.

2 Ye saints rejoice; the Saviour reigns!
  Let praise your tongues employ ; ·
Floods, clap your hands ; exult, ye plains,
  And shout, ye hills, with joy!

3 No more shall sins and sorrows grow,
    Nor thorns o'erspread the ground;
  He comes to make His blessings flow,
    Far as the curse is found.

4 Joy to the world ! the Lord is come !
    Let earth receive her King ;
  Let every heart prepare Him room,
    And all creation sing.

CCXCI.—6, 6, 8, 6.

1 Soon righteousness shall come,
    And dwell on earth again:
  Jesus Jehovah be the King,
    And o'er the nations reign.

2 Jesus Himself shall rule,
    The world shall hear His word ;
  By one bless'd name shall He be known,—
    The Universal Lord.

CCXCII.—8s.

1 FROM all that dwell below the skies,
Let the Creator's praise arise;
Let the Redeemer's name be sung,
Through ev'ry land, by ev'ry tongue.

2 Eternal are Thy mercies, Lord!
Eternal truth attends Thy Word;
Thy praise shall sound from shore to shore,
'Till suns shall rise and set no more.

CCXCIII.—6, 6, 8, 6.

1 WHO trust unto the Lamb,
Whom we in heaven see,
Are cleans'd by blood from guilt and shame,
From condemnation free.

2 In counsels deep of old,
The sons of God they were;
And all the lambs of Jesu's fold
Were blest in Jesus there.

3 This union ne'er shall break,
Though earth's strong columns bow;
The strong, the tempted, and the weak,
Are one in Jesus now.

4 Then, saints, erect your heads,
    You're form'd in Christ anew;
And tho' thro' earth destruction spreads,
    No danger reaches you.

5 Should storms of trouble rise,
    Or deadly foes assail;
Your anchor safe on Jesus lies,
    Your hope's within the vail.

CCXCIV.—8s.

1 Awake, prophetic harp, awake!
Retune thy strings for Jesus' sake;
We sing the Saviour of our race,
The Lamb, our shield and hiding-place.

2 'Tis He, the Lamb, to Him we fly,
While the dread tempest passes by;
God sees His Well-beloved's face,
And spares us in our hiding-place.

3 Thus, while we dwell in this blest scene,
The Lamb is our unfailing screen;
To Him, though guilty, still we run,
And God still spares us for His Son.

4 While yet we sojourn here below,
Pollutions still our hearts o'erflow;
A fall'n, abject, sentenc'd race,
We deeply need a hiding-place.

5 But pure, immortal, sinless, free,
We, through the Lamb, at length shall be;
Shall meet the Father face to face,
And need no more a hiding-place.

CCXCV.—10, 10, 11, 11.

1 THOUGH dark be our way, since God is our
Guide,
'Tis ours to obey; 'tis His to provide:
Tho' cisterns be broken, and creatures all fail,
The Word He hath spoken shall surely prevail.

2 His love in time past forbids us to think
He'll leave us at last in trouble to sink:
The Lamb in His glory is ever in view,
The pledge and the proof He will help us quite
through.

3 And since all we meet must work for our
good,
The bitter is sweet, the med'cine is food;

Though painful at present, 'twill cease before
   long,
And then, how triumphant the conqueror's
   song!

CCXCVI.—6, 6, 8, 6.

1 Our Father! we believe,
   And trust Thy firm resolve:
  The Son has surely done the work,
     That did on Him devolve.

2 His work is all complete—
   Salvation is secure:
  The merits of His life and death,
     Eternally endure.

3 The proof is fix'd in heaven,
   High on Thy glorious throne;
  For Jesus sits beside Thee now,
     Because Thy will is done.

CCXCVII.—8, 8, 6.

1 O Love divine, how sweet Thou art,
   When shall I find my longing heart
     All taken up by Thee?

O may I pant, and thirst to prove
The greatness of redeeming love,
The love of Christ to me!

2 God only knows the love of God,
O that it were more shed abroad
In each poor longing heart!
For love I'd sigh, for love I'd pine;
This only portion, Lord, be mine,
Be mine, this better part!

3 O that I may for ever sit
Like Mary, at the Master's feet!
Be this my happy choice;
My only care, my only bliss,
My joy, my heav'n on earth be this,
To hear the Bridegroom's voice.

4 O that I may, like favor'd John,
Recline my wearied soul upon
The dear Redeemer's breast;
From care and sin, and sorrow free,
Give me, O Lord, to find in Thee,
My everlasting rest!

CCXCVIII.—8s.

1 O MAY we always ready stand,
With our lamps burning in the hand;
May we in sight of heaven rejoice,
Until we hear the Bridegroom's voice!

2 Shine on us, Lord; new life impart;
Fresh ardour kindle in each heart:
And make Thine own all-quick'ning light
Dispel the sloth and clouds of night!

CCXCIX.—8, 8, 6.

1 HAD we ten thousand gifts beside,
We'd cleave to Jesus crucified,
And build on Him alone;
For no foundation is there given,
On which to place our hopes of heaven,
But Christ, the corner-stone.

2 Possessing Christ, we all possess,
Wisdom, and strength, and righteousness,
And sanctity complete.
Bold in His name, we dare draw nigh,
Before the Ruler of the sky,
And all His justice meet.

CCC.—7, 6.

1 O Jesus, gracious Saviour,
   Upon the Father's throne,
Whose wond'rous love and favour
   Have made our cause Thine own;
Thy people to Thee ever
   For grace and help repair,
For Thou they know wilt never
   Refuse their griefs to share.

2 O Lord, through tribulation
   Our weary journey lies,
Through scorn and sore temptation,
   And watchful enemies;
'Midst never-ceasing dangers
   We through the desert roam,
As pilgrims here and strangers,
   We seek the rest to come.

3 O Lord, Thou too once hasted
   This weary desert through,
Once fully tried and tasted
   Its bitterness and woe;
And hence Thy heart is tender,
   In truest sympathy,

Though now the heavens render
All praise to Thee on high.

4 O by Thy Holy Spirit
    Reveal to us Thy love,
The joy we shall inherit
    With Thee, our Head above :
May all this consolation
    Our trembling hearts sustain—
Sure—though through tribulation—
    The promis'd rest to gain.

CCCI.—8, 6.

1 O LORD, when we the path retrace
    Which Thou on earth hast trod,
To man Thy wond'rous love and grace,
    Thy faithfulness to God.

2 Thy love, by man so sorely tried,
    Prov'd stronger than the grave ;
The very spear that pierced Thy side
    Drew forth the blood to save.

3 Faithful amidst unfaithfulness,
  'Midst darkness only light,
Thou didst Thy Father's name confess,
  And in His will delight.

4 Unmoved by Satan's subtle wiles,
  Or suffering, shame and loss,
Thy path, uncheered by earthly smiles,
  Led only to the Cross.

5 O Lord, with sorrow and with shame,
  We meekly would confess,
How little we who bear Thy name,
  Thy mind, Thy ways express.

6 Give us Thy meek, Thy lowly mind,
  We would obedient be,
And all our rest and pleasure find
  In learning, Lord, of Thee.

CCCII.—8, 6, 8, 6, 8, 8, 8, 8.

1 THERE is a place of endless joy
  Prepar'd for saints above,
Of peace and bliss without alloy,
  A heav'n of perfect love:

T

It was for this that Jesus died,
That we with Him might there abide ;
It was for this He suffer'd pain,
That all His saints might with Him reign.

2 How bright, how holy is the place,
  Unfading, undefiled,
Where God unveils His smiling face
  On Jesus His beloved Child—
They round the throne triumphant stand,
A golden harp in ev'ry hand,
To which they sing the ceaseless strain :
" Worthy the Lamb, for sinners slain !"

3 O wondrous grace ! O love divine !
  To give us such a home !
Let us the present things resign,
  And seek this Rest to come—
And gazing on our Saviour's cross,
Esteem all else but dung and loss ;
Press forward till the race be run,
Fight till the crown of life be won.

CCCIII.—8s.

1 *Lord, we are Thine :* our God Thou art,
  Fashioned and made we are by Thee—

303

These curious frames !—in ev'ry part,
   Thy wisdom, power, and love we see,—
Each breath we draw, each pulse that beats,
   Each organ formed by skill divine,
Each precious sense aloud repeats—
   Great God, that we are only *Thine.*

2 *Lord, we are Thine :* in Thee we live,
   Supported by Thy tender care,
Thou dost each hourly mercy give ;
   Thine earth we tread, we breathe Thine air;
Raiment and food Thy hands supply;
   Thy sun's bright rays around us shine ;
Guarded by Thine all-seeing eye—
   We own, that we are only *Thine.*

3 *Lord, we are Thine :* bought by Thy blood,
   Once the poor guilty slaves of sin,
But Thou redeemedst us to God,
   And mad'st Thy Spirit dwell within ;
Thou hast our sinful wand'rings borne,
   With love and patience all divine ;
As brands, then, from the burning torn,
   We own that we are *wholly Thine.*

4 *Lord, we are Thine :* Thy claims we own—
   Ourselves to Thee we wholly give ;

Reign Thou within our hearts alone,
  And let us to Thy glory live ;
Here let us each Thy mind display,
  In all Thy gracious image shine ;
And haste that long expected day,
  When Thou shalt own *that we are Thine.*

CCCIV.—10, 10, 11, 11.

1 COME, saints, praise the Lamb, His mercies
    proclaim,
  And lift up your heads, and sing of His name ;
  His love to the Church, which He purchased
    with blood,
  To make her His Bride and the Temple of
    God.

2 When wand'ring far from the Father's abode,
  The heart full of pride, and hatred to God,
  The children of darkness, of Satan the slaves,
  'Tis Jesus redeem'd us—His merit that saves.

3 Our sins on the cross He on Calv'ry bore,
  He blotted them out, and they are no more ;

Now pardon'd and washed, we spotless appear,
And cry " Abba Father !" unhinder'd by fear.

4 Despised by the world, we're strangers be-
low,
But called to heav'n, we cheerfully go ;
The Lord is our Leader ; and, strong in His
might,
Tho' Satan opposes, we 'll fight the good fight.

5 We look for the day when Jesus shall come,
And fetch all His blood-purchas'd brethren
home ;
When we shall behold all His glory and
grace,
And a heav'n be found in the light of His
face.

CCCV.—7s.

1 WHEN along life's thorny road,
Faints the soul beneath its load,
By its cares and sins opprest,
Finds on earth no peace or rest ;
When the wily tempter 's near,
Filling us with doubts and fear ;

305

Jesus—to Thy feet we flee,
Jesus—we will look to Thee,

2 Thou, our Saviour, from the throne,
List'nest to Thy people's moan ;
Thou, the living Head, dost share
Ev'ry pang the members bear
Full of tenderness Thou art,
Thou wilt heal the broken heart ;
Full of power, Thine arm shall quell
All the rage and might of hell.

3 Thou, O Jesus, Thou hast borne
Satan's rage—the worldling's scorn ;
Thou hast known the bitter hour,
Of the wily tempter's power ;
Lo, Thy bloody sweat we see,
In the dark Gethsemane !
Hark ! that piercing awful cry,
From the Mount of Calvary.

4 By that *Love* which brought Thee down
From Thy high eternal throne,
Veiled the Lord of earth and skies,
In an infant's lowly guise ;
By that *Love* which healed the maim,
Cured the sick, restored the lame,

Bade the darken'd eye to see,
Jesus, we will look to Thee !

5 By Thy tears o'er Lazarus shed,
By Thy power to raise the dead,
By Thy meekness under scorn,
By Thy stripes and crown of thorn ;
By that rich and precious blood,
That hath made our peace with God ;
Jesus—to Thy feet we flee,
Jesus—we will cling to Thee.

6 Mighty to redeem and save,
Thou hast overcome the grave ;
Thou the bars of death hast riv'n,
Open'd wide the gates of heav'n ;
Soon in glory Thou shalt come,
Taking Thy poor pilgrims home ;
Jesus, then we all shall be,
Ever—ever—Lord, with Thee.

CCCVI.—8, 6, 8, 6, 7, 7, 7, 7.

1 BEHOLD yon bright and countless throng,
Around the throne above,
And hearken to their ceaseless song
Of Jesu's dying love:

From the rising of the sun,
Unto where his course is done,
Out of ev'ry land they came,
All who loved the Saviour's name.

2 Behold the robes so dazzling white,
    In which array'd they stand;
Like victors from a glorious fight,
    Palms waving in their hand:
Out of sorrow, toil, and shame,
Gladly borne for Jesus' name;
In His blood their robes made white,
In His strength they won the fight.

3 Behold they strike their golden lyres,
    How sweet, how loud the song!
All heaven's vast angelic choirs,
    In united strain prolong.
" Glory be to Him, Who gave
His dear Son our souls to save;
Glory to the Lamb, Whose blood
Reconciled us all to God !"

4 Soon we shall join that countless throng,
    Safe in the heav'nly fold,
And sing that new, that happy song,
    And wear our crowns of gold.

Let us glory in the cross,
Count all else but worthless dross,
And amidst reproach and shame,
Praise our Jesu's precious name.

CCCVII.—8s.

1 O HAPPY day ! when first we felt
Our souls with true contrition melt ;
And all our sins of crimson guilt
Were cleansed by blood on Calv'ry spilt.

2 O happy day ! when Jesus' love
Began our grateful hearts to move,
And gazing on the wond'rous cross,
We saw all else as worthless dross.

3 O happy day ! when, sin no more,
We meet Him Whom our souls adore ;
When sorrows, conflicts, fears, shall cease,
And all our trials end in peace.

4 O happy day! when we shall see,
And cast our longing eyes on Thee ;
On Thee our light, our life, our love,
Our *all* below, our heaven above.

5 O happy day of cloudless light!
 Eternal day without a night!
 Lord, when shall we its dawning see,
 And spend it all in praising Thee?

6 Come, Saviour, come! O quickly come!
 Take us Thy waiting people home;
 We long to stand around Thy throne,
 To love and serve Thee, Lord, alone.

CCCVIII.—8, 6.

1 LORD Jesus, are we *one* with Thee?
  O height, O depth of love!
 One with us on the cursed tree,
  We *one* with Thee above?

2 Such was Thy grace, that for our sake
  Thou didst from heav'n come down,
 Our mortal flesh and blood partake,
 . In all our misery *one*.

3 Our sins, our guilt, in love divine,
  Confess'd and borne by Thee;
 The gall, the curse, the wrath were Thine,
  To set Thy members free.

4 Ascended now, in glory bright,
　　Still *one* with us Thou art ;
　Nor life, nor death, nor depth, nor height,
　　Thy saints and Thee can part.

5 O teach us, Lord, to know and own
　　This wondrous mystery,
　That Thou with us art truly *one,*
　　And we are *one* with Thee.

6 Soon, soon shall come that glorious day,
　　When, seated on Thy throne,
　Thou shalt to wond'ring worlds display:
　　That Thou with us art ONE !

CCCIX.—10, 10, 11, 11.

1 WE 're not of the world which fadeth away,
　We 're not of the night, but children of day;
　The chains that once bound us, by Jesus are
　　riv'n,
　We 're strangers on earth, and our home is
　　in heav'n.

2 Our path is most rugged, and dang'rous too,
　A wide trackless waste our journev lies
　　through ;

But the Pillar of Cloud that shews us our way,
Is our sure light by night, and shades us by
 day.

3 Our Shepherd is still our Guardian and Guide,
Before us He goes to help and provide ;
We drink of the streams from the Rock that
 was riv'n,
Our bread is the Manna that came down from
 heav'n.

4 Mid mightiest foes—most feeble are we—
Yet trembling in ev'ry conflict they flee ;
The Lord is our Banner—the battle is His—
The weakest of saints more than conqueror is.

5 Soon shall we enter our own promis'd land,
Before His bright throne in glory shall stand :
Our song then for ever and ever shall be,
" All glory and blessing, Lord Jesus, to Thee !"

CCCX.—7, 6.

1 SEE, He comes, He won the day!
 Go ye forth to meet Him ;

Bring the palm, and strew the way,
  And with singing greet Him.
Jesus is the victor's name,
  Jesus, Lord of glory!
Fly, ye heralds, spread His fame,
  Tell the joyful story.

2 Well His people now may sing,
  Sing with exultation;
Since the victor is their King,
  And He brings salvation.
Make the Saviour's triumph known,
  Let the nations hear it;
He alone deserves the crown,
  He alone shall wear it.

CCCXI.—6, 6, 8, 6.

1 Soon shall our Master come,
  Our toil and sorrow cease;
He'll call His waiting servants home,
  And all be joy and peace.

2 *Now* may we do His will,
  In all His footsteps tread;
And, in a world of evil, still
  To grieve Him only dread.

3 May we His name confess
'Midst suffering, shame, and loss;
Stand forth His faithful witnesses,
And glory in the Cross.

4 Watchful may each be found,
Our loins well girded be;
In works of faith and love abound,
Till we our Master see.

5 Then shall we soar above,
Nor cease our sweet employ;
And hear Him say, with tend'rest love,
"*Enter Thy Master's joy.*"

CCCXII.—8, 8, 6.

1 GREAT God, as *Father* Thee we claim,
And bless the Son's most precious name,
Thro' Whom this grace is giv'n;
Who bore the curse to sinners due,
Who form d our ruin'd souls anew,
And made us heirs of heav'n.

2 'Tis by the Holy Ghost alone,
That Jesus Christ is made our own,
The Gift of Grace divine.

But since to us in Jesu's face
There shines the Glory of Thy Grace,
  We know that we are Thine.

3 Then while we here together join,
Before the throne of Grace Divine,
  Bow down a Father's ear;
And while we listen to Thy word,
Or praise Thy name with glad accord,
  Amongst us, Lord, appear.

CCCXIII.—8s.

1 Who then shall God's elect condemn ?
  Since Jesus for their ransom died;
Rising, He intercedes for them,
  And they in Him are justified.

2 Not tribulation, nakedness,
  The famine, peril, or the sword,
Nor persecution nor distress,
  Shall separate from Christ the Lord.

3 Nor life, nor death, nor depth, nor height,
  Nor powers below, nor powers above,
Nor present things, nor things to come
  Can change His purposes of love.

4 His sovereign mercy knows no bounds,
 His faithfulness shall still endure;
And those who on His word rely,
 Shall find this truth for ever sure.

CCCXIV.—8s.

1 O DRAW me, Saviour, after Thee,
 So shall I run, and never tire :
With gracious words still comfort me,
 Be Thou my hope, my sole desire ;
Free me from every weight : nor fear,
Nor sin can come, if Thou art near.

2 What in Thy love possess I not ?
 My star by night, my sun by day,
My spring of life, when parch'd with drought,
 My wine to cheer, my bread to stay,
My strength, my shield, my safe abode,
My robe before the throne of God !

3 From all Eternity with love
 Unchangeable Thou hast me viewed ;
Ere knew this beating heart to move,
 Thy tender mercies me pursued :
Ever with me may they abide,
And close me in on every side.

315

CCCXV.—8, 6.

1 AWAKE, ye saints, awake and watch,
   The Bridegroom may be near;
How awful, should His coming catch
   His people slumb'ring here!

2 They who are ready to attend
   The Lord when He appears,
With Him to glory shall ascend;
   Eternal life is theirs.

3 With Him they shall sit down, and feast
   On heav'n's unbounded store;
Enjoy an everlasting rest,
   And never hunger more.

4 When once the chamber door shall close,
   'Tis sure beyond a doubt,
No further hope remains for those
   Who then are found without.

5 Awake, and be ye like to those
   Who wait their Lord's return;
Awake, nor yield to that repose,
   Whose end it is to mourn.

U

CCCXVI.—8, 7.

Jesus comes by crowds attended,
  Heav'n the dazzling train supplies:
Call the dead; the night is ended;
  Bid the sleeping dust arise:
    Let the ransom'd
  Join the Saviour in the skies.

2 'Tis the day so long expected;
  Shout, ye saints, and triumph now;
See your Lord, by man rejected;
  Many crowns adorn His brow;
    'Tis His triumph:
  Ev'ry knee to Him shall bow.

CCCXVII.—8s.

1 Jesus, we hail Thee Israel's King;
  To Thee our tribute, Lord, we bring;
  Nor do we fear to bow the knee;
  They worship God, who worship *Thee.*

2 Hail! Israel's King, enthron'd in light,
  Whose glory never shone more bright
  Than when, by faithless friends betray'd,
  Thy foes insulting homage paid.

3 Then did admiring angels see
  Divine forbearance, Lord, in Thee;
  With emphasis pronounce Thee *good;*
  And heav'n and earth contrasted stood.

4 An object of contempt beneath,
  And judg'd by men to suffer death;
  By angels own'd, admir'd, ador'd,
  The great, the everlasting Lord!

5 Reign, mighty Lord, for ever reign!
  Thy cause throughout the world maintain;
  Let Israel's God His triumphs spread,
  And crowns of glory wreath His head!

CCCXVIII.—7, 7, 7, 7, 8, 8.

1 *Sing aloud to God, our strength;*
    He has brought us hitherto;
  He will bring us home at length;
    This the Lord our God will do:
  Doubt not, for His word is stable;
  Fear not, for His arm is able.

2 *Sing aloud to God, our strength;*
    Sing with wonder of His love;

Who can tell its breadth and length?
　Who below, or who above?
Who its depth and height can measure?
'Tis a rich unbounded treasure!

3 *Sing aloud to God, our strength;*
　He is with us where we go;
Fear we not the journey's length,
　Fear we not the mighty foe:
All our foes shall be defeated,
And our journey be completed.

CCCXIX.—8, 7, 8, 7, 7, 7.

1 In our Lord we have redemption,
　Full remission in His blood;
From the curse entire exemption,
　From the curse pronounc'd by God:
What a Saviour Jesus is!
O what love, what love is His!

2 Praise be His, all praise transcending,
　Praise on earth, and praise in heav'n;
Praise through ages never-ending,
　To the Lamb of God be giv'n:
He alone the Saviour is,
Everlasting praise be His.

CCCXX.—8s.

1 Ours is a pardon bought with blood,
　　Amazing truth ! the blood of One
Who, without usurpation, could
　　Lay claim to heav'n's eternal throne.

2 No victim of inferior worth
　　Could ward the stroke that justice aim'd;
For none but He, in heav'n or earth,
　　Could offer that which justice claim'd.

3 But He, the Lord of glory, came;
　　On yonder cross He bow'd His head;
He suffer'd pain, He suffer'd shame,
　　And lay a pris'ner with the dead.

4 But lo ! He rises from the grave,
　　And bears the greatest, sweetest name ;
The Lord, almighty now to save,
　　From sin, from death, from endless shame.

CCCXXI.—8, 7.

1 Saviour, through the desert lead us,
　　Without Thee we cannot go ;

Thou from cruel chains hast freed us,
  Thou hast laid the tyrant low:
    Let Thy presence
  Cheer us all our journey through.

2 With a price Thy love has bought us,
    (Saviour, what a love is Thine!)
  Hitherto Thy pow'r has brought us,
    (Pow'r and love in Thee combine):
      Lord of glory,
    Ever on Thy household shine.

3 Through a desert waste and cheerless,
    Though our destin'd journey lie,
  Render'd by Thy presence fearless,
    We may ev'ry foe defy:
    · Nought shall move us,
    While we see the Saviour nigh.

4 When we halt, (no track discov'ring),
    Fearful lest we go astray,
  O'er our path Thy pillar hoy'ring,
    Fire by night, and cloud by day,
      Shall direct us ;
    Thus we shall not miss our way.

5 When we hunger, Thou wilt feed us,
    Manna shall our camp surround ;

Faint and thirsty, Thou wilt heed us,
 Streams shall from the Rock abound:
  Happy people !
 What a Saviour have we found !

6 When our foes in arms assemble,
 Ready to obstruct our way,
Suddenly their hearts shall tremble,
 Thou wilt strike them with dismay ;
  And Thy people,
 Led by Thee, shall win the day. .

7 Then lead on, Almighty Victor,
 Scatter ev'ry hostile band ;
Be our guide and our protector,
 Till on Canaan's shores we land :
  Where in glory
 Soon we hope with Thee to stand.

CCCXXII.—8, 7.

1 Rise, my soul, thy God directs thee,
 Stranger hands no more impede ;
Pass thou on, His hand protects thee,
 Strength that has the captive freed.

2 Is the wilderness before thee,
 Desert lands where drought abides ?

322

Heavenly springs shall there restore thee,
    Fresh from God's exhaustless tides.

3 Light divine surrounds thy going,
    God Himself shall mark thy way,
Secret blessings, richly flowing,
    Lead to everlasting day.

4 God, thine everlasting portion,
    Feeds thee with the mighty's meat,
Price of Egypt's hard extortion,
    Egypt's food no more to eat.

5 Art thou wean'd from Egypt's pleasures?
    God in secret thee shall keep,
There unfold His hidden treasures,
    There His love's exhaustless deep.

6 In the desert God will teach thee
    What the God that thou hast found,
Patient, gracious, powerful, holy,
    All His grace shall there abound.

7 On to Canaan's rest still wending,
    E'en thy wants and woes shall bring
Suited grace from high descending,
    Thou shalt taste of mercy's spring.

8 Though thy way be long and dreary,
   Eagle strength He 'll still renew:
Garments fresh, and foot unweary
   Tell how God hath brought thee through.

9 When to Canaan's long-loved dwelling
   Love divine thy foot shall bring,
There with shouts of triumph swelling
   Zion's songs in rest to sing:

10 Then no stranger God shall meet thee,
   Stranger thou in courts above,
He who to His rest shall greet thee,
   Greets thee with a well-known love.

CCCXXIII.—8, 7.

1 WOULD we view God's brightest glory,
   We must look in Jesu's face;
Sing, and tell the pleasing story,
   O ye sinners sav'd by grace;
     And with pleasure,
   Bid the guilty Him embrace.

2 In His highest work, redemption,
   See His glory fully blaze·

324

Nor can angels ever mention
  Aught that more of God displays;
  Grace and justice
  Here unite to endless days.

3 In the person of the Saviour,—
  God's full majesty is seen;
  Love and justice shine for ever;
  And, without a veil between,
  Man may meet Him,
  And rejoice in His great name.

4 O how true and blest the pleasure,
  God to view in Christ the Lord;
  There He smiles, and smiles for ever;
  Let the church this truth record;
  Praise and bless Him!
  And His wonders spread abroad.

CCCXXIV.—6, 6, 4, 6, 6, 6, 4.

1 SINCE Thou, my Lord, art nigh,
  Foes I may well defy,
    Strong is Thine arm;
  Since grace and truth are Thine,
  Wisdom and love divine—
  Triumph and peace are mine:
    Nothing shall harm.

2 Nothing shall greatly move
Those who Thy kindness prove,
  Blessed alone;
Strong their Redeemer is,
Greatness and grace are His,
This, and far more than this,
  Lord, is Thine own.

3 Then let Thy favour be
Dearer than life to me,
  Be Thy name dear;
When foes against me fight,
Then raise Thine arm of might,
Then save Thy worm from flight,
  Save him from fear.

CCCXXV.—7, 7, 8, 7 bis

1 THY name we bless, Lord Jesus,
That name all names excelling,
  How great Thy love
  All praise above,
Should ev'ry tongue be telling.
The Father's loving-kindness,
In giving Thee was shewn us;
  Now by Thy blood
  Redeem'd to God,
As children He doth own us.

325

2 From that eternal glory
  Thou hadst with God the Father,
    He sent His Son
    That He in one,
  His children all might gather;
  Our sins were all laid on Thee,
  God's wrath Thou hast endured;
    It was for us
    Thou suff'redst thus,
  And hast our peace secured.

3 Thou from the dead wast raised—
  And from all condemnation
    Thy Church is free,
    As ris'n in Thee,
  Head of the new creation!
  On high Thou hast ascended,
  To God's right hand in heaven,
    The Lamb once slain,
    Alive again,—
  To Thee all power is given.

4 Thou hast bestow'd the earnest
  Of that we shall inherit;
    Till Thou shalt come
    To take us home,
  We're seal'd by God the Spirit.

We wait for Thine appearing,
When we shall know more fully,
The Priest and King
Whose praise we sing,
Thou Lamb of God most holy!

CCCXXVI.—8s.

THOU, LAMB OF GOD! didst shed Thy blood
Thou didst our load of misery bear ;
And hast exalted us to share
The rank of Kings and Priests to God.
To Thee we render evermore
The honour, glory, praise that's due ;
Might, power, and obedience, too,
And in our hearts we Thee adore.
Amen ! Amen !
O Lord, Amen !

CCCXXVII.—8, 8, 6, bis.

1 O JESUS ! everlasting God !
Who didst for sinners shed Thy blood
Upon the shameful tree ;
And finish there redemption's toil,
And win for us the happy spoil,
All praise we give to Thee.

2 Fain would we think upon Thy pain,
  Would find therein our life and gain,
    And firmly fix the heart
  Upon Thy grief and dying love,
  Nor evermore from Thee remove,
    Though from all else we part.

3 The more through grace ourselves we know,
  The more rejoic'd we are to bow
    And glory in Thy cross;
  To trust in Thine atoning blood,
  And look to Thee for ev'ry good,
    And count all else but loss.

CCCXXVIII.—8s.

1 Jesus for us a body took,
  Our guilt assum'd, our bondage broke,
  Discharging all our dreadful debt;
  Then let us ne'er this love forget?

2 Let us renounce our ways with grief,
  And cleave to this most sure relief;
  Nor Him forget Who left the throne,
  And for our life gave up His own.

3 Ah no! till time itself depart,
His name shall cheer and warm each heart;
And, shouting this, from earth we'll rise
To join the chorus of the skies.

4 Ah no! when all things else expire,
And perish in the general fire,
His name all others shall survive,
And through eternity shall live.

CCCXXIX.—8s.

1 O Saviour! can it ever be
That we should be asham'd of Thee?
And not with joy Thy name confess
Before Thy proudest enemies?

2 Asham'd of Jesus—Lamb of God,
Who freed us by His precious blood;
Of Him, Who to retrieve our loss
Despis'd the shame, endur'd the cross.

·3 Asham'd of Jesus—of that friend
Whose love to us can know no end!

It must not be—this be our shame
That we no more confess His name.

4 The world's anointed King and Lord,
  By all the hosts of heav'n ador'd!
  Yes! we will make our boast of Thee,
  Now, and to all eternity.

5 And when we stand before Thy throne,
  Thou wilt confess us as Thine own,—
  And, for the world's rejecting frown,
  Give to each saint a royal crown.

CCCXXX.—8, 8, 6, bis.

1 O THOU Who hast redeem'd of old,
  And made me of Thy grace take hold,
    And be at peace with Thee,
  Help me these blessings now to own,
  And tell aloud what Thou hast done,
    O Holy Lamb, for me.

2 O Thou incarnate Deity,
    Who hast Thy love vouchsaf'd to me,
      Thy love 's the plea I make,

Give me this pow'r, 'tis all I claim,
With heart and life to serve Thy name,
    Give, for Thy mercy's sake.

3 Love, only love, Thy heart inclin'd,
And brought Thee, Saviour of mankind,
    Down from the throne above ;
Love made Thee here a man of grief,
Distress'd Thee sore for our relief,
    O mystery of love !

4 Then since Thou, Lord, didst die for me,
Cause me, my Saviour, to love Thee,
    And gladly to resign
Whate'er I have, whate'er I am,
My life be all with Thine the same,
    And all Thy shame be mine.

CCCXXXI.—8s.

1 His mournful days of flesh are o'er,
    Accomplish'd is His sacrifice,
He suffer'd once, but dies no more,
    Nor adds to that stupendous price,
Which purchas'd for the faithful race
Pardon, and peace, and holiness.

x

2 All who are call'd by grace as His,
    Out of this evil world He takes,
And renders meet for endless bliss,
    Partakers of His nature makes ,
And crowns with all the joy above,
Their patient faith, and humble love.

CCCXXXII.—7, 6.

1 We go to meet the Saviour,
    His glorious face to see ;
What manner of behaviour
    Doth with this hope agree ?
May God's illumination,
    Guide heart and hand aright ;
That so our preparation
    Be pleasing in His sight.

2 We'd gladly wile the hours,
    Till night shall pass away,
And chant with all our powers
    The blessings of that day ;
To Thee, the King of glory,
    We'd raise the happy song,
And make Thy love's bright story
    The theme of ev'ry tongue.

3 This caus'd Thine incarnation,
   This brought Thee from on high,
Thy thirst for our salvation,
   This made Thee come to die ;
O love beyond all measure,
   Wherewith Thou didst embrace
The victims of the pressure
   Of sin and its disgrace !

4 Not sinful man's endeavour,
   Nor any mortal's care,
Could draw Thy sov'reign favour
   To sinners in despair ;
Uncall'd Thou cam'st with gladness,
   Us from the fall to raise,
And change our grief and sadness,
   To songs of joy and praise.

CCCXXXIII.—8, 6.

1 To us, our God His love commends,
   When by our sins undone ;
That He might spare His enemies,
   He would not spare His Son,—

2 His only Son, on whom He plac'd
   His whole delight and love,

Before He form'd the earth below,
Or spread the heav'ns above.

3 Our sorrows and our sins to bear,
Our heavy cross sustain ;
Upon the tree He came to die,
That we might life obtain.

4 This life is hid in God with Him,
Who fell a sacrifice,
And dying, conquer'd death for us,
That we, .ike Him, might rise.

5 Quickly He triumph'd o'er the grave,
And went to heav'n again ;
There intercedes, and thence will come
With all His saints to reign.

6 His word assures He'll quickly come—
For this His brethren pray ;
The whole creation for it groans,
Come, Lord, without delay.

CCCXXXIV.—7, 7, 8, 7, bis.

1 THOU God of grace, our Father!
We now rejoice before Thee ;
Thy children we,
And lov'd by Thee,
'Tis meet we should adore Thee!

334

As Thine Thou didst foreknow us,
For such was Thine election,
    And Thou hast shewn
    To us " Thine own"
Thy fulness of affection.

2 Thou didst in Jesus choose us
Before the world's foundation ;
    Ere Adam's fall
    Involv'd us all
In guilt and condemnation.
Thy purpose and election,
In spite of all our failing,
    Have firmly stood,
    And by the blood
Of Christ are made availing.

3 The grace of Thy salvation
The Holy Ghost hath taught us ;
    By Him we 're seal'd,
    For He reveal'd
How Jesu's blood hath bought us.
Soon, all the church in glory,
In its predestin'd station,
    Shall bless Thy name,
    With Christ " The Lamb,"
Thou God of our salvation !

CCCXXXV.—8s.

1 REJOICE, ye saints, rejoice and praise
  The blessing of redeeming grace;
  Jesus, your everlasting tow'r,
  Mocks at the angry tempest's roar.

2 His love's a refuge ever nigh,
  His watchfulness, a mountain high;
  His name's a rock, which winds above
  And waves below can never move.

3 His faithfulness for ever sure,
  For endless ages will endure;
  His perfect work will ever prove
  The depth of His unchanging love.

4 While all things change, He changes not,
  He ne'er forgets, though oft forgot;
  His love's unchangeably the same,
  And as enduring as His name.

5 Rejoice, ye saints, rejoice and praise
  The blessings of this wondrous grace;
  Jesus, your everlasting tow'r,
  Can bear unmov'd the tempest's roar.

CCCXXXVI.—8s.

1 Poor, weak, and worthless, though I am,
  I have a rich Almighty friend,
Jesus, the Saviour, is His name,
  He freely loves, and without end.

2 He ransom'd me from hell with blood,
  And by His pow'r my foes controll'd ;
He found me wand'ring far from God,
  And brought me to His chosen fold.

3 He cheers my heart—my want supplies,
  And says that I shall shortly be
Enthron'd with Him above the skies:
  O what a friend is Christ to me !

CCCXXXVII.—8, 6.

1 O gracious Father! God of love !
  We own Thy pow'r to save,—
That pow'r by which our Shepherd rose
  Victorious o'er the grave.

2 Him from the dead Thou brought'st again,
  When, by His sacred blood
Confirm'd and seal'd for evermore,
  Th' eternal cov'nant stood.

3 O let Thy Spirit seal our souls,
  And mould them to Thy will,
That from Thy paths we ne'er may stray,
  But keep Thy precepts still !

4 That to perfection's sacred height
  We nearer still may rise ;
And all we think, and all we do,
  Be pleasing in Thine eyes.

CCCXXXVIII.—8s.

1 O that we never might forget
  What Christ has suffer'd for our sake,
To save our souls, and make us meet
  Of all His glory to partake ;
But keeping this in mind, press on
To glory and the victor's throne.

2 But, gracious Lord, when we reflect
  How oft we've turn'd the eye from Thee,
And treating Thee with sad neglect,
  Have listen'd to the enemy,
And yet to find Thee still the same—
'Tis this that humbles us with shame.

3 Astonish'd at Thy feet we fall,
  Thy love exceeds our highest thought,

Henceforth be Thou our all in all,
  Thou Who our souls with blood hast bought;
May we henceforth more faithful prove,
And ne'er forget Thy ceaseless love.

CCCXXXIX.—8, 8, 6.

1 FROM various cares our hearts retire,
  Though deep and boundless their desire,
    We're now to please but One;
  He, before Whom the elders bow,
  With Him is all our bus'ness now,
    And those that are His own.

2 With these our happy lot is cast,
  Through the world's deserts rude and waste,
    Or through its gardens fair;
  Whether the storms of trouble sweep,
  Or all in dead supineness sleep,
    T' advance be all our care.

3 O Lord, our way, our truth, our life!
  Let sin and sorrow, doubt and strife,
    Drop off like autumn leaves;
  And may we, privileg'd by Thee,
  Simple and undistracted be,
    The church which to Thee cleaves.

4 Let us the weary mind recline
 On that eternal love of Thine,
   And human thoughts forget ;
 Child-like attend what Thou wilt say,
 Go forth and serve Thee while 'tis day,
   Yet leave not our retreat.

CCCXL.—8s.

1 JESUS, Who vanquish'd all our foes,
   Who came to save, Who reigns to bless,
 From Thee our ev'ry comfort flows,
   Life, liberty, and joy, and peace.
 Resound, ye saints, the joyful strain,
 Let Him, the King of glory, reign.

2 O Thou art worthy, gracious Lord,
   Of universal, endless praise,
 With ev'ry pow'r to be ador'd
   That men or angels e'er can raise.
 And heav'n and earth shall blend their strains,
 Jesus, the King of glory, reigns.

3 But earth and heav'n can ne'er proclaim
   The boundless glories of their King;
 Yet do our hearts adore His name,
   The name whence all our blessings spring.

341

Resound, resound the joyful strain,
Let Him, the King of glory, reign.

4 How mean the tribute that we pay!
   How cold the heart, how faint the tongue!
But O a bright eternal day
   Will bring a more exalted song,
Resounding in immortal strains,
Jesus, the King of glory, reigns!

CCCXLI.—8s.

1 SALVATION's Captain, and the guide
   Of all that seek the rest above,
Beneath Thy shadow we abide,
   The cloud of Thy protecting love;
Our strength Thy grace, our rule Thy word,
Our end, the glory of our Lord.

2 By Thine unerring Spirit led,
   We shall not in the desert stray,
Or light for our direction need,
   Or lose, though dark and drear, our way,
But kept from danger, and from fear,
Since Thine Almighty love is near.

CCCXLII.—8s.

1 STRANGERS and pilgrims here below,
   This earth we own not as our place,
But hasten through its toil and woe,
   Impatient to behold Thy face;
On to our heav'nly country move,
Our everlasting home above.

2 We 've no continuing city here,
   But seek a city out of sight,
Thither our upward course we steer,
   As dwellers in its courts of light;
Jerusalem, the saints' abode,
Whose builder is the living God.

3 Patient, th' appointed race we run,
   This weary world we cast behind,
From strength to strength we travel on,
   Our holy dwelling-place to find;
Our labour this, our only aim,
To reach the new Jerusalem.

CCCXLIII.—8, 7.

1 CROSS, reproach, and tribulation,
   Of the church are certain guests,

When she has this consolation,
   That on Christ alone she rests.

2 The reproach of Christ is glorious—
   All who here His burden bear,
In the end will prove victorious,
   And eternal glories share.

3 Christ, the ever blessed Saviour,
   Bore for us reproach and shame;
Now as conqu'ror lives for ever,
   And we conquer in His name.

4 Bear we, then, reproach for Jesus,
   Living still a life of faith;
Let us sing glad songs of praises,
   Though it be 'mid shame and death.

CCCXLIV.—8s.

1 O ISRAEL, to thy tents repair,
   Why so secure on hostile ground?
The King commands thee to beware,
   For many foes thy camp surround.

2 The trumpet sounds a martial strain,
   Then Israel gird thee for the fight;
Arise, the combat to maintain,
   And put thine enemies to flight.

3 Thou should'st not sleep as others **do**,
   Awake, be vigilant, be brave ;
The coward and the sluggard too,
   Must wear the fetters of the slave.

4 A nobler lot is cast for thee,
   Fair Canaan 's spread before thine eyes:
With such a hope, shall Israel flee ?
   Or yield through weariness the prize ?

5 No, though a careless world repose,
   And slumber on through life's short day,
God's Israel to the conflict goes,
   And bears the glorious prize away.

CCCXLV.—8, 6.

1 WE tread the path our Master trod,
   What can we wish for more ?
And ev'ry thorn that wounds our feet
   His temples pierc'd before.

2 Our Shepherd's pow'r is always near,
   His arm outstretch'd in love !
And while our bodies wander here,
   Our hearts are fix'd above.

3 Afflictions purge our dross away,
   Refining as we run ;
And, while we die to earth and sense,
   Our heav'n is here begun.

CCCXLVI.—8, 8, 6.

1 ABOVE the clouds a city stands,
   Of living stones not made with hands,
      Where God the Saviour 'll reign :
'Tis built for sinners bought with blood,
Redeem'd and sanctified to God,
      And cleans'd from every stain.

2 The cities of this world must fall,
   However solid, they must all
      The common ruin share;
But yonder city still appears
Unchangeable through endless years,
      For God Himself is there.

3 Happy the saints who shall abide
   Within those walls, and there reside
      For ever with the King ;
We hope that we shall soon be there,
Its joys and blessedness to share,
      The Saviour's praise to sing.

CCCXLVII.—8s.

1 AH! who upon earth can conceive
  The bliss that in heaven Saints share?
Or who this dark world would not leave,
  And earnestly long to be there?
There Christ is the light and the sun,
  His glories unhinder'dly shine;
His presence their spirits have won,
  And rest in the glory divine.

2 'Tis good, at His word, to be here,
  Yet better it is to be gone,
And there in His presence appear,
  And rest as He rests on the throne;
Yet ah! it will gladden our eyes,
  When Him we behold on the cloud,
And echo the joys of the skies,
  And shout to the trumpet of God.

CCCXLVIII.—8s.

1 WHAT will it be to dwell above,
  And with the Lord of glory reign,
Since the sweet earnest of His love,
  So brightens all this dreary plain:
No heart can think, no tongue explain,
  What joy 't will be with Christ to reign.

2 When sin no more obstructs our sight,
    And flesh and sense deceive no more,
When we shall see the Prince of light,
    And all His works of grace explore:
What heights and depths of love divine,
Will there through endless ages shine!

3 And God has fix'd the happy day,
    When the last tear shall dim our eyes,
When He will wipe these tears away,
    And fill our hearts with glad surprise;
To hear His voice, and see His face,
And feel His infinite embrace.

4 This is the joy we seek to know,
    For this with patience we would wait,
Till call'd from earth and all below,
    We mount to our celestial seat;
To wave our palms, and wear the crown,
And at His feet to cast them down.

CCCXLIX.—8, 6.

1 Soon on this wretched scene of night
    Unbounded bliss shall rise,
And realms of infinite delight
    Shall gladden mortal eyes.

350

2 There pain and sickness ne'er shall come,
   There man shall ne'er complain ;
But all who reach that peaceful home,
   With Jesus there shall reign.

3 No cloud that region e'er shall know
   For ever bright and fair ;
For sin, the source of mortal woe,
   Can never enter there.

4 O may the heav'nly vision fire
   Our hearts with ardent love,
Till wings of faith and strong desire
   Bear ev'ry thought above.

CCCL.—8s.

1 HAIL, blessed scene of endless joy !
   Where Jesus shall for ever reign,
Where nothing hurtful shall annoy,
   But gladness fill the happy plain :
Free from all sin, and free from fear,
None shall e'er sigh or shed a tear.

2 Ten thousand thousands then shall raise
   Their joyful notes, and sing this strain ;

Awake the song of grateful praise,
  Unto the Lamb Who once was slain.
Hosannas, loud hosannas sing,
Hosannas to th' eternal King.

3 For ever there with Jesus blest,
  They fear no death, and feel no pain,
But there shall be in endless rest,
  Where dangers ne'er shall threat again;
For Jesus reigns, and they shall share
With Him His fullest glory there.

CCCLI.—8s.

1 The countless multitude on high,
  That tune their songs to Jesu's name,
All merit of their own deny,
  And Jesu's worth alone proclaim.

2 Firm on the ground of sov'reign grace,
  They stand before Jehovah's throne.
The only song in which blest place
  Is—"Thou art worthy! Thou alone!"

3 With spotless robes of purest white,
  And branches of triumphal palm,

351

They shout, with transports of delight,
 Heaven's ceaseless universal psalm :—

4 " Salvation's glory all be paid
 To Him Who sits upon the throne ;
And to the Lamb, Whose blood was shed,
 Thou ! Thou art worthy ! Thou alone !"

5 " For Thou wast slain, and in Thy blood
 These robes were wash'd so spotless pure ;
Thou mad'st us kings and priests to God—
 For ever let Thy praise endure."

6 While thus the ransom'd myriads shout,
 " Amen," the holy angels cry ;
" Amen, Amen," resounds throughout
 The boundless regions of the sky.

7 Let us with joy adopt the strain
 We hope to sing for ever there ;
" Worthy's the Lamb for sinners slain,
 Worthy alone the crown to wear !"

8 Without one thought that's good to plead,
 O what could shield us from despair
But this, though we are vile indeed,
 The Lord our Righteousness is there.

CCCLII.—6, 6, 8, 6.

1 To heaven's eternal King
　The praise of saints be giv'n;
His name, His glorious name we sing,
　The rightful Heir of heav'n.

2 He once was found with men,
　A man of sorrows He;
He bore His people's sentence then,
　He bore it on the tree.

3 He suffer'd in their stead,
　He sav'd His people thus;
The curse that fell upon His head,
　Was due, by right, to us.

4 'Twas love that brought Him down,
　The purest, strongest love;
He bore the cross, He won the crown,
　And now He reigns above.

5 The praise of saints be given
　To Him Who worthy is;
He died on earth—He lives in heav'n,
　Eternal praise be His.

CCCLIII.—8, 6.

1 Though now we bear the chilly blast,
   Though cradled now in woe,
The church shall ev'ry storm outlast,
   Outlive each cruel foe.

2 Then shall we sing of battles won,
   Of garments roll'd in blood,
Of myriads slain by David's Son,
   The conq'ring Lamb of God;

3 Of blood that loos'd the captive's chain,
   Redeem'd his life, and seal'd
The record of a deathless name
   That lives in heav'n reveal'd.

CCCLIV.—8s.

1 See mercy, mercy from on high,
Descend to rebels doom'd to die;
'Tis mercy free, which knows no bound;
How sweet, how blessed is the sound!

2 Soon as the reign of sin began,
The light of mercy dawn'd on man,
   Then God announc'd the early news,
   he woman's seed Thy head shall bruise."

3 Brightly it beam'd on men forlorn,
　When Christ, the holy child was born;
　And brighter still in splendour shone,
　When Jesus, dying, cried, " 'Tis done !"

4 The work complete when He arose,
　Bursting the snares of all His foes,
　When captive led captivity,
　And took for us His seat on high.

5 Till we around Him then shall throng,
　This mercy shall be still our song;
　And ev'ry scheme shall God confound
　Of all who strive its course to bound!

CCCLV.—8, 6.

1 AWAKE our souls ! awake our tongues;
　　The subject is divine:
　The Saviour's love demands our songs :
　　Let all His people join.

2 This Saviour is the Mighty God,
　　Who rests in heav'n above ;
　Reveal'd in flesh, He shed His blood,
　　And thus declar'd God's love.

3 Jesus, Thy love exceeds our thought;
   But this at least we see,
The soul that knows Thy pow'r is taught
   To value nought but Thee.

4 And though Thy love be faintly seen,
   What 's seen demands our praise;
Without it, Lord, we still had been
   Engag'd in folly's ways.

CCCLVI.—8, 7.

1 Sov'REIGN grace o'er sin abounding!
   Ransom'd souls the tidings swell,
'Tis a deep that knows no sounding;
   Who its breadth or length can tell?

2 Sav'd by Christ, we 're free for ever,
   This the Spirit's voice declares!
Death, nor hell, nor sin shall sever,
   Jesus from the chosen heirs.

3 Saints above, in His communion,
   Rest from conflict with their Head;
  'e we sing the blessed union,
   ough in thorny paths we tread.

CCCLVII.—8, 6.

1 To the Redeemer's glorious name
   Awake the sacred song !
   O may His love (immortal flame !)
   Tune every heart and tongue.

2 His love what human thought can reach ?
   What tongue on earth display ?
   Imagination's utmost stretch
   In wonder dies away.

3 Let wonder still with love unite,
   And gratitude with joy ;
   Jesus be our supreme delight,
   His praise our blest employ.

4 Jesus, Who left the throne on high,
   Left the bright realms of bliss,
   And came to earth to bleed and die:
   Was ever love like this ?

5 Dear Lord, we gladly, humbly pay
   Our grateful thanks to Thee,
   For, taught of God, we each can say,
   " The Saviour died for me.'

CCCLVIII.—11s.

THY mercy, O God! is the theme of my song,
The joy of my heart, and the boast of my tongue;
'Tis free grace alone, from the first to the last,
Can win the affections, and bind the soul fast.

CCCLIX.—11s.

LORD Jesus! we worship and bow at Thy feet,
And give Thee the glory, the praise that is meet;
While, through Thee, to God our hosannas arise,
And swell the full chorus that gladdens the skies.

CCCLX.—8, 6.

1 JESUS! O name divinely sweet!
   How charming is the sound!
What joyful news, what heavenly pow'r
   In Thy dear name is found.

2 Our souls, as guilty and condemn'd,
   In hopeless fetters lay
Our souls with numerous sins deprav'd,
   To death and hell a prey.

3 Jesus, to purge away this guilt,
 A willing victim fell,
And on His cross triumphant broke
 The bands of death and hell.

CCCLXI.—8s.

1 O Love divine, Thou vast abyss!
 My sins are swallow'd up in Thee;
Cover'd is my unrighteousness;
 From condemnation I am free.
While Jesu's blood through earth and skies,
"Mercy! free, boundless mercy!" cries.

2 Fix'd on this ground must I remain,
 Though my heart fail and flesh decay;
This anchor shall my soul sustain,
 When earth's foundations melt away:
Mercy's full pow'r I then shall prove,
Lov'd with an everlasting love.

CCCLXII.—7s.

1 Blessed are the sons of God!
 They are bought with Jesu's blood;
 They are ransom'd from the grave;
 Life eternal they shall have.

2 God did love them in His Son
 Long before the world begun;

They the seal of this receiv'd
When on Jesus they believ'd.

3 They are lights upon the earth,
Children of an heav'nly birth;
Born of God, they hate all sin,
God's pure seed remains within.

4 They have fellowship with God
Through the Mediator's blood:
One with God, with Jesus one,
Glory is in them begun.

5 They alone are truly bless'd,
Heirs of God, joint heirs with Christ;
Blessed this fraternity,
Here and in eternity!

CCCLXIII.—7s.

1 BRETHREN, while we sojourn here,
Fight we must, but should not fear;
Foes we have, but we 've a Friend,
One that loves us to the end.
Forward, then, with courage go,
Long we shall not dwell below;
Soon the joyful news will come,
" Child, your Father calls—Come home "

2 In the way a thousand snares
  Lie, to take us unawares;
  Satan, with malicious art
  Watches each unguarded part;
  But, from Satan's malice free,
  Saints shall soon victorious be;
  Soon the joyful news will come,
  "Child, your Father calls—Come home."

3 But, of all the foes we meet,
  None so oft mislead our feet,
  None betray us into sin
  Like the foes that dwell within:
  Yet let nothing spoil your peace,
  Christ will also conquer these;
  And the joyful news will come,
  "Child, thy Father calls—Come home."

CCCLXIV.—8, 8, 6 bis.

1 BEHOLD the temple of the Lord!
  God's building, where, by saints ador'd,
    His presence He reveals:
  Jehovah-Jesus, God of peace,
  Rears it to be His resting place,
    And there His glory dwells.

2 A temple this not made with hands,
   The workmanship of grace it stands,
       And ever shall endure:
   'Tis founded on the " Living Stone,"
   And mid all changes shall be known,
       Immutably secure.

3 Time, that all other work destroys,
   Combin'd with power that hell employs,
       With safety it defies :
   Erected for God's own name's sake,
   Though earth with deep convulsions shake,
       Majestic it shall rise.

4 Age after age the work goes on ;
   Soon shall we hear the voice, " 'Tis done,"
       And hail its crowning stone ;
   With all the armies of the sky,
   " Grace! Grace unto it !" we shall cry
       And Jesu's praise make known.

CCCLXV.—PECULIAR.

1 O Thou that dwell'st in the heavens high,
   Above yon stars, and within yon sky,
   Where the dazzling fields never needed light,
   Of the sun by day, nor the moon by night!

2 Tho' shining myriads around Thee stand,
   For the sake of Him at Thy right hand;
   O think of those that cost Him dear,
   Still left 'mid death and darkness here!

3 Our night is dreary, and dim our day;
   And if Thou turnest Thy face away,
   We are sinful, feeble, and helpless dust,
   We have none to look to, and none to trust.

4 The pow'rs of darkness are all abroad,
   They ask no Saviour, they seek no God;
   And us they scorn who await the day—
   Then turn not Thou Thy face away!

5 A life of scorn for us Thou didst lead,
   And in the grave laid'st Thy blessed head;
   Then grant us grace, undauntedly
   To lay down life and all for Thee.

6 Thine aid, O mighty One, we crave,
   Nor shortened is Thine arm to save,
   Afar from Thee we now sojourn—
   Return to us, O Lord, return!

CCCLXVI.—8s.

To glory in Jesus, we think
   Our duty and joy evermore, -

For He is our meat and our drink,
  Our life, and our strength, and our store ;
Our Shepherd, our Husband, our Friend,
  Our Saviour from sin and from thrall ;
Our hope from beginning to end,
  Our portion, our Lord, and our all.

CCCLXVII.—8, 7.

1 LOVE divine, all loves excelling,
    Joy of Heav'n, to earth come down!
  Bless us with Thy rich indwelling,
    All Thy faithful mercies crown !
  Jesus, Thee we'd still be blessing,
    Serve Thee as Thy hosts above,
  Praise Thee, Saviour, without ceasing,
    Glory in Thy dying love.

2 Carry on Thy new creation—
    Faithful, holy, may we be,
  Joyful in our full salvation,
    Perfectly conform'd to Thee !
  Changed from glory into glory,
    'Till in heav'n we take our place,
  Then we'll cast our crowns before Thee,
    Lost in wonder, love and praise !

CCCLXVIII.—8, 6.

1 SEE how within the holiest
  The blessèd Saviour stands;
There He prepares for us a place,
  With incense from His hands.

2 Brethren! His glory all is ours,
  His fellowship with God,
Yes, there we sit in Christ the Lord,
  Fruit of His precious blood!

CCCLXIX.—8, 7.

1 JESUS in the heav'nly temple
  Sits with God upon the throne,
Now no more to be forsaken,
  His humiliation gone.

2 Dwelling in eternal sunshine
  Of the countenance of God;
There He fills the heav'ns with incense
  Of His reconciling blood.

3 With this wondrous Christ we are one,
  Being of the Spirit born;

And of God belov'd in Jesus,
  We can love Him in return.

CCCLXX.—8, 7.

1 PRINCE of life, and first-born brother
    Of the chosen family,—
  Brightness of the Father's glory,
    All Whose fulness dwells in Thee,—
      God and kinsman,
    We extol Thy majesty.

2 Gladly with Thee we will suffer,
    Since we hope with Thee to reign ;
  Keep us, then, as servants mindful
    Of our Master's toil and pain,
      Till we see Thee,
    In Thy glory, come again.

CCCLXXI.—8, 7.

1 Go, and search the tomb of Jesus,
    Where the Lord of Glory lay ;
  Jesus is not there, but risen,
    And has borne our sins away,
      It is finish'd !
    Captive leads captivity.

2 Could not all our sins retain Him,
   Prison'd in the guarded cave?
No, He conquer'd death in dying,
   By His cross He spoil'd the grave:
      Lo! He 's risen!
   Yes, the Lord is risen indeed.

CCCLXXII.—8s.

1 O GLORIOUS grace! nor spot nor stain
   Is seen on the adopted child;
Jesus, Who died and rose again,
   The holy, harmless, undefil'd,
Within the Holiest is gone,
And stands before the Father's throne.

2 The Saviour died upon the tree,
   And sank for us beneath the flood;
Our sins are drown'd as in a sea
   Of love, of sorrow, and of blood!
Perfect in Jesu's sacrifice,
Her foes the blameless church defies.

3 Then, God, we give Thee of Thine own,
   Hearts by Thy Jesu's cross subdued,
Polluted once, and hearts of stone,
   But by Thy Spirit now renew'd;

Look on, Thou glorious Priest and King,
While we to God this off'ring bring.

CCCLXXIII.—8, 7.

1 Now the throne of God the Father
    Jesus crucified requites;
Where exalted, crown'd with glory,
    In the church He still delights.

2 Come, behold Him, our forerunner,
    Gone within the holy place,
Heaven itself the holy temple,
    There He sees the Father's face.

  As the eye of God the Father
    Ever loves on Christ to rest;
So, by God, are all His members
    In their Head belov'd and blest.

CCCLXXIV.—8s.

1 God's tender mercies follow still,
    Each step of our appointed race;
In weakness now we do His will,
    But hope to see Him face to face.

2 Then God shall wipe all tears away,
 As we are known, we then shall know,
Nor shall we from those fountains stray,
 Whence living waters ceaseless flow.

CCCLXXV.—6, 6, 8, 6.

1 'Tis finish'd! wondrous word!
 The Son of God is slain;
Jehovah's mercy-seat appears,
 The vail is rent in twain.

2 Now truth and mercy meet
 In holy unity,
Since Jesu's blood the ransom is,
 That sets the pris'ner free.

3 Within the holy place
 Made by Jehovah's hands,
There Jesus, Who was crucified,
 In kingly priesthood stands.

4 There He in heaven appears,
 For us to intercede;
And countless benefits proclaim,
 "The Lord is risen indeed."

CCCLXXVI.—8, 7.

1 HOLY SAVIOUR! we adore Thee,
   Seated on the throne of God;
While the heav'nly hosts before Thee,
   Gladly sing Thy praise aloud.
     " Thou art worthy!
   We were ransom'd by Thy blood."

2 Saviour! though the world despis'd Thee,
   Though Thou here wast crucified,
Yet the Father's glory rais'd Thee,
   Lord of all creation wide;
     " Thou art worthy!
   We shall live, for Thou hast died."

3 And though here on earth rejected,
   'Tis but fellowship with Thee,
What besides could be expected,
   Than like Thee our Lord to be?
     " Thou art worthy!
   Thou from earth hast set us free."

Haste the day of Thy returning,
   With Thy ransom'd church to reign;

Then shall end our days of mourning,
We shall sing with rapture then,
" Thou art worthy !"
" Come, Lord Jesus, Come.   Amen !"

CCCLXXVII.—8, 7.

1 FATHER ! we, Thy children, bless Thee,
For Thy love on us bestow'd,
As our Father we address Thee,
Call'd to be the sons of God.
Wondrous was Thy love in giving
Jesus for our sins to die,
Wondrous was His grace in leaving,
For our sakes, His home on high.

2 Now the sprinkled blood has freed us,
On we go toward our rest,
Through the desert Thou dost lead us,
With Thy constant favour blest:
By Thy truth and Spirit guiding,
Earnest He of what's to come,
And with daily food providing,
Thou dost lead Thy children home.

3 Though our pilgrimage be dreary,
This is not our resting-place ;

Shall we of the way be weary,
   When we see our Master's face ?
Now, by faith anticipating,
   In this hope our souls rejoice,
We, His promised advent waiting,
   Soon shall hear His welcome voice.

4 Father, O how vast the blessing,
   When Thy Son returns again ⟨
Then Thy saints, their rest possessing,
   O'er the earth with Him shall reign ;
For the fathers' sakes beloved,
   Israel, in Thy grace restor'd,
Shall on earth, the curse removed,
   Be the people of the Lord.

5 Then shall countless myriads, wearing
   Robes made white in Jesu's blood,
Palms (like rested pilgrims) bearing,
   Stand around the throne of God:—
These, redeem'd from every nation,
   Shall in triumph bless Thy name;
Every voice shall cry "Salvation,
   To our God, and to the Lamb !"

SPECIAL OCCASIONS

MORNING.

1.—8s.

1 AWAKE, my soul, and with the sun
Thy daily stage of duty run:
Shake off dull sloth, and early rise
To pay thy morning sacrifice.

2 Glory to Thee, Who safe hast kept,
And hast refresh'd me while I slept!
Guard the first springs of thought and will,
And with Thyself my spirit fill.

3 Direct, control, suggest this day
All I may think, or do, or say;
That all my powers, with all their might,
For Thy sole glory may unite.

4 Heaven, Lord, is there where'er Thou art;
O never then from me depart;
For to my soul 'twere hell, to be
But for one moment void of Thee.

5 Praise God from Whom all blessings flow,
Praise Him, all creatures here below:
Praise Him above, ye heav'nly host,
Praise Father, Son, and Holy Ghost.

B

2.—8, 6.

1 LORD of my life, O may Thy praise
    Employ my noblest pow'rs ;
  Whose goodness lengthens out my days,
    And fills the circling hours.

2 Preserv'd by Thine almighty arm,
    I pass'd the shades of night,
  Serene, and safe from every harm,
    And·see returning light.

3 While many spent the night in sighs,
    And restless pains and woes ;
  In gentle sleep I clos'd mine eyes,
    And undisturb'd repose.

4 When sleep, death's semblance, o'er me spread,
    And I unconscious lay,
  Thy watchful care was round my bed,
    To guard my feeble clay.

5 O let the same almighty care
    My waking hours attend ;
  From every danger, every snare,
    My trembling steps defend.

6 Smile on the minutes as they roll,
    And guide my future days ;
  And let Thy goodness fill my soul
    With gratitude and praise.

3.—8, 6.

1 LORD, for the mercies of the night,
    My grateful thanks I pay,

And unto Thee I dedicate
　The first-fruits of the day.

2 Let this day praise Thee, O my God !
　And so let all my days;
And O let mine eternal day
　Be Thine eternal praise.

4.—8, 6.

1 THROUGH all the dangers of the night,
　Preserv'd, O Lord, by Thee,
Again we hail the cheerful light,
　Again we bow the knee.

2 O may the beams of truth divine,
　With pure convincing light,
In all our understandings shine,
　And clear our mental sight.

3 Preserve us, Lord, throughout the day,
　And guide us by Thine arm ;
For *they* are safe, and *only* they,
　Whom Thou dost keep from harm.

4 Let all our words and all our ways
　Declare that we are Thine ;
That so the light of truth and grace
　Before the world may shine.

5 Nor let us turn away from Thee ;
　Dear Saviour, hold us fast,
Till with immortal eyes we see
　Thy glorious face at last.

5.—8s.

1 In sleep's serene oblivion laid,
   I safely pass'd the silent night;
   Again I see the breaking shade,
   I drink again the morning light.

2 Refresh'd, I bless the waking hour,
   Once more, with awe, rejoice to *be ;*
   My conscious soul resumes her power,
   And springs, my Saviour God, to Thee !

3 O guide me through the various maze,
   Which I and Thine are forced to tread ;
   And spread Thy shield's protecting blaze,
   Where dangers press around my head.

EVENING.

6.—8s.

1 Glory to Thee, my God, this night,
   For all the blessings of the light;
   Keep me, O keep me, King of kings,
   Under Thine own Almighty wings.

2 Forgive me, Lord, for Thy dear Son,
   The ills that I this day have done ;
   That with the world, myself, and Thee,
   I, ere I sleep, at peace may be.

3 O may my soul on Thee repose,
   And with sweet sleep mine eyelids close;
   Sleep, that may me more active make,
   To serve my God when I awake.

4 Should death itself my sleep invade,
Why should I be of death afraid ?
Protected by Thy saving arm,
Tho' death may strike, it cannot harm.

5 For death is life, and labour rest,
When with Thy gracious presence blest ;
Then welcome sleep or death to me,
I'm still secure, for still with Thee.

6 Praise God, from whom all blessings flow,
Praise Him, all creatures here below:
Praise Him above, ye heav'nly host,
Praise Father, Son, and Holy Ghost !

7.—8, 6.

1 Now Father, let our evening songs
Like holy incense rise ;
And let the off'rings of our tongues
Be holy sacrifice.

2 Through all the dangers of the day
Thyself for us hast car'd ;
And still to drive our wants away,
Thy mercy stands prepar'd.

3 Perpetual blessings from above
Encompass us around ;
But ah ! how few returns of love
Hath our Redeemer found.

4 What have we done for Him Who died
To save our sinful souls ?
Alas ! our sins are multiplied,
Fast as each minute rolls.

5 Yet with these sin-stain'd lives of ours,
    Lord, to Thy blood we flee;
And yield them up with all their powers,
    To be renew'd by Thee.

8.—8, 6.

1 GOD of my life, with grateful heart,
    My ev'ning song I raise;
But, O Thy thousand, thousand gifts
    Exceed my highest praise.

2 What shall I render for the care
    Which me this day has kept?
A thankful heart, though no return,
    Thy grace will still accept.

3 The sins and follies, holy God,
    Which I this day have done,
I would confess with grief; and pray
    For pardon through Thy Son.

4 Much of my precious time I've lost:
    This sinful waste forgive;
And one day nearer now—to Thee,
    Lord, teach me now to live.

9.—8, 7, 8, 7, 7, 7.

1 THROUGH the day Thy love has spar'd us,
    Wearied now we part for rest;
Through the silent watches guard us,
    Let no foe our peace molest:
Jesus! Thou our guardian be,
Sweet it is to trust in Thee.

2 Pilgrims here on earth, and strangers,
   Dwelling in the midst of foes ;
Us, and ours preserve from dangers,
   In Thine arms may we repose:
And when man's sad day is past,
Rest with Thee in heav'n at last.

10.—7, 7, 7, 7, 8, 8.

1 THROUGH the dark and silent hours
   Of the night, preserve us, Lord !
Safely keep both us and ours,
   Peace and confidence afford:
We are bold, in Thee confiding,
Safe beneath Thy shade abiding.

2 Since we cannot tell to-day
   What to-morrow's dawn may bring ;
Saviour, draw our hearts away
   Far from ev'ry earthly thing:
Make us, in Thy service steady,
Always for Thy coming ready.

————

LORD'S DAY MORNING.

11.—8, 8, 8, 4.

1 HAIL ! holy day, most blest, most dear !
   When death's dark region, sad and drear,
   Those strange mysterious sounds did hear,
      " The Lord is risen."

2 The holy Captive's bonds are riven,
To Him the keys of death are given,
Be glad, O earth, and shout, O heaven!
    " The Lord is risen."

3 Shall this triumphant theme inspire
The angel's song, the seraph's lyre,
And saints not sing with such a choir,
    " The Lord is risen"?

4 For not for them His life He gave;
He did not die their souls to save;
It is for man that from the grave
    " The Lord is risen."

5 For man He left His glorious throne,
For man to death's dark realm went down;
And now to heaven for man alone
    " The Lord is risen!"

12.—8, 6.

1 THE Risen Lamb, come let us praise,
    In concert with the blest;
Who, joyful in harmonious lays,
    Employ an endless rest.
Thus, Lord, while we remember Thee,
    We bless'd and patient grow;
And learn by hymns of praise to be
    Triumphant here below.

2 On this glad day a brighter scene
    Of glory was display'd,
By God, the eternal Word, than when
    This universe was made:

For then He rose, the church Who bought
  With grief and pain extreme:
'Twas great to speak a world from nought;
  'Twas greater to redeem.

13.—8, 6.

1 MAY we throughout this day of Thine
  Be in Thy Spirit, Lord,
And full of humble fear divine,
  That trembles at the word.

2 And full of faith, each heart to raise,
  And fix on things above,
And full of sacrifice and praise,
  Of holiness and love.

LORD'S DAY.

14.—8, 6.

1 THIS is the day, the blessed day
  When Jesus left the grave:
Of Him we sing, and well we may,
  For us He came to save.

2 'Tis sweet to know that by His death
  We live—this grace is sweet:
The Saviour, with His dying breath,
  Proclaim'd His work complete.

3 He lives, He reigns the God of love,
  He reigns for evermore:

His pow'r, all other pow'rs above,
His name, all names before.

4 To Him Who died and rose again,
The Lord of earth and heav'n;
To Him by angels and by men,
Be endless glory giv'n.

5 The glory due to Him alone,
Who reigns in heaven above:
Who fills the everlasting throne,
The God of grace and love.

15.—7s.

1 GLAD this day, the first of sev'n,
Glad we sing, " The Lord is ris'n,"
Christ our King, the Lord from heav'n,
Rose this day, and left His pris'n.

2 Left the grave, awhile His pris'n.
Left it, to return no more:
Sing we then, " The Lord is ris'n,"
Sing His name, Whom saints adore.

3 Since He rose, His saints shall rise;
Since He lives, His saints shall live:
Theirs are everlasting joys,
All is theirs that grace can give.

16.—8, 6.

1 THE week's first day is that on which
The Saviour left the grave:
We sing of Him in mercy rich;
His arm is strong to save.

2 He drank a bitter cup for us,
   How bitter, who can tell?
'Twas thus He paid our debt, and thus
   He saved our souls from hell.

3 We hail the day, the week's first day,
   The day the Saviour rose:
The Lord, He bore our sins away;
   From this our comfort flows.

4 From this there flows a rich supply
   Of all we can require;
Tis pardon, peace, and holy joy—
   What more can we desire?

5 What more, but that we may sustain
   Untir'd the holy strife;
And then, with all the victors, gain
   A crown, the crown of life?

17.—8, 6.

1 THE day that Jesus rose should be
   Remember'd by His friends;
Upon His rising, all agree,
   Their hope of heaven depends.

2 If Jesus rose not from the dead,
   His people's hope is vain;
He then would have no power to save,
   Nor should they live again.

3 But now is Jesus ris'n indeed,
   And He " the first-fruits" is;
The first-fruits of the ransom'd seed,
   Of those He claims as His.

4 As He is ris'n, so they shall rise;
  As He lives, so shall they:
A dwelling theirs beyond the skies,
  And theirs a glorious day.

5 The hope that Jesus shall appear,
  And take His saints to heav'n,
To dwell with Him for ever there;
  This hope to saints is giv'n.

18.—8, 8, 8, 7.

1 On this day, the first of seven,
Sinners we, through grace forgiven,
Come before the God of heaven:
  Saviour, let us hear Thy voice.

2 From our hearts remove all sadness;
Fill us, Lord, with holy gladness:
All the worldling's mirth is madness;
  But Thy people should rejoice.

3 Of Thy love for ever tasting,
Theirs are pleasures everlasting;
Theirs a treasure never wasting,
  Which nor moth nor rust destroys.

4 Trusting to Thy faithful promise,
Joy and gladness well become us:
Who shall wrest the blessing from us,
  Who that force or guile employs?

19.—7s.

1 Blessed day, the first of sev'n!
  'Tis the day when Jesus rose;

And, with Him, the heirs of heav'n:
  Blessed day, when saints repose !

2 Blessed day, when Christians meet,
  Breaking bread in peace and love,
Sitting at the Saviour's feet,
  Drawing comforts from above !

3 Jesus died, and rose again ;
  Jesus took His place above:
Heaven was fill'd with rapture then ;
  All was wonder, joy, and love.

4 Sing we then of Him Who died,
  Him Who rose again and lives ;
Sing of Jesus glorified,
  Him Who all our sin forgives ;

5 Him Who saves us by His grace,
  Keeps us till the final day ;
Gives us then a glorious place:
  Sing of Him, for well we may.

20.—7s.

1 CHRIST the Lord is risen to-day,
Sons of men and angels say ;
Raise your songs of triumph high,
Sing ye heav'ns, and earth reply.

2 Love's redeeming work is done,
Fought the fight, the battle won ;
Lo! our sun's eclipse is o'er,
Lo! He sets in blood no more.

3 Vain the stone, the watch, the seal,
   Christ hath burst the gates of hell,
   (Death in vain forbids His rise),
   He hath opened Paradise.

4 What tho' once we perish'd all,
   Partners of our parents' fall;
   Second life we now receive,
   And in Christ for ever live.

————

LORD'S DAY EVENING.

21.—7s.

1 ERE our evening meeting's close,
   Ere again we seek repose,
   Lord, our song ascends to Thee,
   While we gladly bow the knee.

2 For the mercies of this day,
   For refreshment on our way,
   Thanks to Thee alone be given,
   Lord of earth and God of heaven.

3 Cold our services have been,
   Mingled every prayer with sin;
   But Thou canst and dost forgive;
   For by grace alone we live.

4 Whilst this thorny path we tread,
   May Thy love our footsteps lead;
   While their steps Thy pilgrims bend
   To the rest which knows no end.

CHRISTIAN SABBATH.

22.—8, 6.

"For we which have believed do enter into rest."—
Heb. iv. 3., con. Mat. xi. 23—30.

1 I REST in Christ the Son of God,
   Who took the servant's form;
By faith I flee to Jesu's cross,
   My covert from the storm.

2 At peace with God, no ills I dread,
   The cup of blessing mine;
The Lord is risen, His precious blood
   Is new and living wine.

3 Jesus put all my sins away
   When bruised to make me whole:
Who shall accuse or who condemn
   My blameless ransom'd soul?

4 O thou destroyer, see the blood
   That makes the guilty clean,
No prey of thine the soul on which
   This token once is seen.

LORD'S SUPPER.

23.—8s.

"For I have received of the Lord that which also I
delivered unto you, That the Lord Jesus, the *same* night
in which he was betrayed, took bread: And, when he had
given thanks, he brake it, and said, Take, eat: this is my
body, which is broken for you: this do in remembrance

of me. After the same manner also *he took* the cup, when
he had supped, saying, This cup is the new testament in
my blood : this do ye, as oft as ye drink *it*, in remembrance of me. For as often as ye eat this bread, and
drink this cup, y e do shew the Lord's death till he come."
—1 Cor. xi. 23—26.

1 OFT we, alas ! forget the love
    Of Him Who bought us with His blood ;
Who now, as our High Priest above,
    E'er intercedes for us with God.

2 Oft we forget the woe, the pain,
    The bloody sweat, th' accursed tree,
The wrath His soul did once sustain,
    From sin and death to set us free.

3 Oft we forget that, strangers here,
    This world is not our rest or home ;
That, waiting till our Lord appear,
    Our hearts should cry, " Come, Saviour,
        come !"

4 Oft we forget that we are *one*
    With every saint that loves His name ;
United to Him on the throne—
    Our life, our hope, our Lord, the same.

5 O, then, what love is here display'd !
    That Jesus did this feast provide
The very night He was betray'd,
    The very night before He died.

6 Here, in the broken bread and wine,
    We hear Him say, " Remember me !
" I gave My life to ransom thine,
    "I bore thy curse to set thee free."

7 Lord, we are Thine—we praise Thy love—
　One with Thy saints, all one in Thee;
We would, until we meet above,
　In all our ways, *remember Thee.*

24.—7s.

1 JESUS, once for sinners slain,
　From the dead was raised again;
And in heav'n is now set down,
Glorious on His Father's throne.

2 He has made an end of sin,
And His blood has wash'd us clean;
In our midst, assembled here,
Jesus stands His saints to cheer.

3 While we break the bread in faith,
We shew forth our Saviour's death;
Bread thus broken aptly shews
How His body God did bruise.

4 While by faith we drink the wine,
Of His blood we see the sign;
Precious blood! so freely spilt,
To redeem our souls from guilt.

5 Lord, we thus remember Thee;
But we long Thy face to see—
Long to reach our heav'nly home.
" Come, Lord Jesus, quickly come!"

25.—6, 6, 8, 6.

1 WE bless our Saviour's name,
　Our sins are all forgiven;

c

To suffer once to earth He came:
He now is crown'd in heaven.

2 His precious blood was shed,
　His body bruis'd for sin;
Remembering this, we break the bread,
　And joyful drink the wine.

3 While we remember Thee,
　Lord, in our midst appear;
Let each by faith Thy body see,
　While we assemble here.

4 We never would forget
　Thy rich, Thy precious love;
Our theme of joy and wonder here,
　Our endless song above.

5 O let Thy love constrain
　Our souls to cleave to Thee!
And ever in our hearts remain
　That word, *Remember me.*

26.—8, 7.

1 See! the Saviour spreads a table,
　And invites His friends to eat:
Surely none but He is able
　To supply so rich a treat:
　'Tis His body:
Brethren, this indeed is meat.

2 Come, and round His board assemble;
　Jesus bids you now draw near:

Ye who hear His word and tremble,
 Banish every servile fear:
  Come and witness
 That the Lord Himself is here.

3 Gracious Master! bless our meeting;
 Grant us spiritual food,
While the world is still repeating,
 "Who will shew us any good?"
  On Thy people
 Shine from heaven Thy bright abode.

27.—8, 7, 8, 7, 7, 7.

1 BRETHREN, come, our Saviour bids us—
 Bids us to a feast of love:
Bless the Lord, Whose bounty feeds us
 With provision from above:
Ye, for whom His life was given,
Come and eat the bread of heaven.

2 Let us think of Him who bought us;
 'Tis the Saviour's own command:
When we wander'd, Jesus sought us;
 Now He leads us by the hand—
Now He gives us hope, and says,
We shall sing His endless praise.

3 O how much His people owe Him!
 O what love our Lord has shewn!
Well may we surrender to Him
 All that once we call'd our own.
Lord, we give ourselves to Thee—
Thou our Guide, our Master be!

28.—6, 8.

1 Jesus invites His saints
   To meet around His board;
Here pardon'd sinners sit and hold
   Communion with their Lord.

2 Our heav'nly Father calls
   Christ and His members one;
We the young children of His love,
   And He the first-born Son.

3 We are but sev'ral parts
   Of the same broken bread;
Our body hath its sev'ral limbs,
   But Jesus is the Head.

4 Let all our pow'rs be join'd,
   His glorious name to raise;
Pleasure and love fill every mind,
   And ev'ry voice be praise.

29.—7s.

1 Meeting in the Saviour's name,
   "Breaking bread" by His command,
To the world we thus proclaim,
   On what ground we hope to stand,
When the Lord shall come with clouds,
Join'd by heaven's exulting crowds.

2 From the cross our hope we draw,
   'Tis the sinner's sure resource;
Jesus magnified the law,
   Jesus bore its awful curse:

What a joyful truth is this!
O how full of hope it is !

3 Jesus died, and then arose—
   Yes, He rose, He lives, He reigns;
Jesus vanquish'd all His foes,
   Jesus led them all in chains:
His the triumph and the crown,
His the glory and renown.

4 Sing we then of Him Who died;
   Sing of Him Who rose again;
By His blood we're justified,
   And with Him we hope to reign;
Yes, we hope to see our Lord,
And to share His bright reward.

30.—8, 6.

1 This is the feast of heavenly wine,
   And God invites to sup;
The juices of the Living Vine
   Were press'd to fill the cup.

2 O bless the Saviour! ye that eat,
   With royal dainties fed;
Not heaven affords a costlier treat,
   For Jesus is the bread.

31.—8, 7.

1 O how sweet, how comfortable,
   In the wilderness to see
Rich provisions, and a table
   Spread for sinners, spread for me!

2 Here Thy bounty still partaking,
    In these signs of bread and wine,
  Freely all things else forsaking,
    I behold the Saviour mine.

3 In His bruised body broken,
    In the shedding of His blood,
  See, my soul, a gracious token,
    Sure and full for ev'ry good.

4 To His cross for refuge flying,
    Arm thee for the strife within;
  There, from Thy Redeemer dying,
    Learn the sinfulness of sin.

5 Cleans'd, and wash'd, and freely pardon'd,
    By His matchless love and power;
  Hear Him say (no longer harden'd),
    " Go in peace, and sin no more."

32.—8s.

1 Ours is a rich and royal feast,
  Provided by the King of heaven:
  How privileg'd are they, and blest,
  To whom the bread of life is given!

2 In sacred fellowship we meet,
  To celebrate our Saviour's death:
  His blood we drink, His flesh we eat;
  His people feed on Him by faith.

3 We worship Him Who bore the cross;
  We glory in His death alone:
  The world itself appears but loss
  To those to whom His name is known.

4 The blood He shed supplies a stream
That washes all our guilt away;
How precious, then, the Lord should seem,
Whose death we celebrate to-day!

5 On earth His dying love shall be
Our spring of hope, our theme of joy;
And, when in heaven our Lord we see,
His praise shall all our pow'rs employ.

33.—8s.

1 Our passover is offer'd up,
The bread we break His body is;
His blood was shed to fill the cup,
And O was ever love like His!

2 The Master of the feast has said,
Be sure all leaven to remove;
And keep it with th' unleaven'd bread
Of truth, sincerity, and love.

3 May we obey, and sweetly prove
How blest they are who know His name;
And share at length, with those above,
The wedding supper of the Lamb.

34.—8, 6.

1 In fellowship we meet around
The table of our Lord;
Let joy and thankfulness abound,
For faithful is His word.

2 The people whom the Lord appoints
The heirs of glory here;

He saves, and by His grace anoints,
  And bids them nothing fear.

3 The food they eat is meat indeed,
  The richest heav'n affords;
The bread of God is living bread,
  His words are living words.

4 Then let our thankful songs abound,
  Our privilege is great;
Our Father's table we surround,
  And eat of children's meat.

35.—8, 7.

" This do in remembrance of me."—Luke xxii. 19.

1 BREAKING bread in love together,
  As our Master bid us do,
We have joy and profit, whether
  Men approve the deed or no;
    Sweet the seasons,
  When our Saviour meets us so.

2 Love is cherish'd and augmented,
  While we keep our Saviour's laws;
And His people are contented
  To forego the world's applause:
    Should they suffer,
  Pain is sweet in such a cause.

3 Saviour, hear Thy people praying,
  Hear us from Thy throne of grace;
O be here, Thy love displaying,
  Let Thy people see Thy face;
    'Tis Thy presence
  Renders sacred ev'ry place.

4 Let us here have sweet communion
  With each other and with Thee ;
Truth the sacred bond of union,
  Truth that makes Thy people free ;
    Heav'n in prospect,
  Heav'n where saints Thy glory see.

36.—8s

7 Obedient to our dying Lord,
  Who bid us thus remember Him,
O let us now surround His board,
  His flesh our food, His love our theme.

2 Sweet feast ! here love and union reign,
  An earnest of the joys above ;
And, meanest of the Saviour's train,
  We celebrate His dying love.

3 O may that love, by pow'r divine,
  To all our hearts be now made known;
Dear Saviour, on Thy people shine,
  The people Thou hast made Thine own.

37.—8, 6

1 Our Saviour's death is here display'd.
  The death endur'd for us:
On Jesus all our sin was laid,
  He bore it on His cross.

2 And now in heav'n His people's names
  Upon His breast appear ;
For them eternal life He claims,
  Whose sin He cancell'd here.

3 We hope with all the ransom'd crowd
  Ere long to see His face;
To testify our joy aloud,
  In songs of endless praise.

38.—8, 8, 6.

1 In blessed union here we meet,
We sit at the Redeemer's feet,
  And eat the bread of heav'n;
How highly privileg'd are we,
And O how thankful should we be,
  To whom this grace is giv'n!

2 To join in fellowship, how sweet,
With those who in the Saviour meet,
  Enlighten'd from above!
How excellent the pleasure is,
That flows from such a feast as this,
  Where all are join'd in love.

3 But if such joy is found to flow
From sacred fellowship below,
  Then what must heaven be?
Where all the Saviour's friends shall meet,
And dwell in happiness complete,
  Throughout eternity.

39.—8s.

1 In sacred fellowship we meet,
  To celebrate our Saviour's death;
His blood we drink, His flesh we eat,
  His people feed on Him by faith.

2 How blest the people who are His!
   To them the bread of life is giv'n;
   How fair, how rich their portion is!
   They hope to see their Lord in heav'n.

3 Till He appear, His death shall be
   Their spring of hope, their theme of joy;
   And when in heav'n their Lord they see,
   His praise shall all their pow'rs employ.

40.—8, 7.

1 O how pleasant, thus united,
   To surround the sacred board!
   While the hosts above, delighted,
   Sing the praises of our Lord;
      Let us join them;
   Be the Saviour's name ador'd.

2 When He died, the cup was finish'd,
   That which He was call'd to take;
   Yes, He drank it undiminish'd,
   Drank it for His people's sake;
      Jesus drain'd it;
   Nothing could His purpose shake.

3 Let us thank Him, let us praise Him,
   Let us sing, though well we know
   Nought of our's can ever raise Him,
   No, nor all that angels do;
      Yet His people
   Should confess how much they owe.

41.—8, 7.

1 At our Father's table meeting,
   All our sins by Him forgiv'n;

Children's bread together eating,
  Bread that cometh down from heav'n;
    Let us banish
  Hence the old unhallow'd leav'n.

2 Blessed is the name we think of,
  When together breaking bread;
Blessed is the cup we drink of,
  Type of blood, for sinners shed:
    Happy are we,
  Quicken'd by the Lord, and fed.

3 Let us walk in love, united
  To our living Head above,
Let us sing His praise delighted,
  Sing the praise of Him we love:
    Saviour, bless us!
  Let us all Thy goodness prove.

4 Standing in the Saviour's merit,
  We have peace, and we are blest;
Taught and guided by the Spirit,
  We have hope of future rest:
    This we wait for,
  And the Saviour's time is best.

42.—8, 6.

1 WHILE we partake the bread and wine,
  As emblems of Thy death,
Lord, raise each soul above the sign,
  To feast on Thee by faith.

2 We do not come as strangers, Lord,
  Who only see the sign,

But, as the objects of Thy love,
   As sav'd by love divine.

43.—7s.

1 O THE matchless love of God;
   He hath bought the church with blood:
   Jesus, her exalted Head,
   For her sigh'd, and groan'd, and bled.

2 She deserv'd eternal pain,
   But the Lamb for her was slain;
   He endur'd the wrath of heav'n
   That her sins might be forgiv'n.

3 He invites us to this feast;
   Bids our souls His glories taste;
   And with pleasure keep in view,
   What He once for us went through.

4 Hear Him speak, ye saved few
   For this word is sent to you;
   You, the objects of His choice,
   Listen to the Saviour's voice:

5 "This, my body is, and blood;
   Take, receive it, as your food;
   But, as oft as this ye do,
   Keep your martyr'd Lord in view.

6 "View Him in the church's place,
   Overwhelm'd in deep disgrace:
   Plung'd in horror's dreadful flood,
   Bearing all the wrath of God.

7 " Risen now, with wonder tell,
  He has vanquish'd death and hell:
  Cancell'd all your sins with blood,
  And will bring you home to God."

8 Shortly He Himself will come,
  And will raise us to His throne;
  Where His glories He'll display,
  Through a long and endless day.

44.—8, 6.

1 THESE emblems of the Saviour's love,
    By faith may we receive;
  And with a solemn pleasure prove,
    That we in Him believe.

2 No goodness of our own we bring;
    For we are vile and base;
  Christ is our all, of Christ we sing,
    And wait to see His face.

3 As beggars poor, and blind, and mean,
    We rest on Christ alone:
  Thanks to the Lamb that once was slain—
    The Lamb that did atone.

4 Our sins are His (O bless His name!)
    His righteousness is our's;
  He saves from Satan, wrath, and sin,
    And all their frightful powers.

5 Then let us each, with heart and tongue,
    Sing, " Worthy is the Lamb !"
  To Him alone the praise belongs,
    And we'll adore His name.

45.—8, 7, 8, 7, 7, 7.

1 See! the Father's hand is spreading
   Manna in the wilderness:
See! the Holy Ghost is shedding
   Love, and joy, and peacefulness:
To Himself, the lost, the vile—
God in Christ doth reconcile.

2 Till we knew *this cup of blessing*,
   Nothing for our souls sufficed:
Here we rest, by faith possessing
   Pardon through the blood of Christ.
Now we thirst for nought beside:
All our wants are satisfied.

3 While we share in sweet communion,
   While on Christ our souls are fed,
Here the world may see our union,
   One the body—*one the bread.*
Now we seek for nought beside,
Richly all our need supplied.

4 In the heav'ns our Lord is seated,
   And His church is in Him there;
When on earth the Bride's completed,
   All His glory we shall share:
But till He, our life, appear,
Nought but suffering know we here.

46.—8, 7.

"The cup of blessing which we bless, is it not the
communion (lit. FELLOWSHIP) of the blood of Christ?
The bread which we break, is it not the communion
(lit. FELLOWSHIP) of the body of Christ? For we,

bring many, are one bread, *and* one body ; for we all are partakers of that one bread."

1 SIMPLY as disciples gather'd
    In His name—The Lord is here;
And in Him our all is treasur'd,
    Him we all in common share.

2 Not to teach or hear assembling,
    But to DO our Master's will;
Thus to Jesu's self resembling,
    God Himself shall cheer us still.

3 Yea, this table of communion,
    Whither by the Lord we 're led,
Sweetly speaks our blessed union,
    One the body—one the bread.

4 And as gather'd round the table,
    We the wine together sup,
We have joy, both sure and stable,
    One the blessing—one the cup.

5 In the Spirit one for ever,
    One with Christ, and one with God;
One we are, and nought can sever
    Us who are redeem'd with blood.

6 By our sins His blood was spilled,
    Pardon hence through love Divine!
And, through Him the law fulfilled,
    In His righteousness we shine.

7 Till He comes we still are thinking
    That " we wait for Him to come,"
And (with us the new wine drinking)
    Take us to His royal home.

47.—8s.

1 Thy broken body, gracious Lord!
   Is shadow'd by this broken bread,
The wine which in this cup is pour'd
   Points to the blood which Thou hast shed.

2 And while we meet together thus,
   We shew that we are one in Thee,
Thy precious blood was shed for us,
   Thy death, O Lord, has set us free.

3 Brethren in Thee, in union sweet,
   (For ever be thy grace ador'd),
'Tis in Thy name, that now we meet,
   And know Thou'rt with us, gracious Lord.

4 We have one hope—that Thou wilt come,
   Thee in the air we wait to see,
When Thou wilt take Thy people home,
   And we shall ever reign with Thee.

48.—8, 6.

1 With Jesus in our midst
   We gather round the board;
Though many, we are one in Christ,
   One body in the Lord.

2 Our sins were laid on Him
   When bruis'd on Calvary;
With Christ we died and rose again,
   And sit with Him on high.

D

3 Faith eats the bread of life,
   And drinks the living wine;
Thus we in love together knit,
   On Jesus' breast recline.

4 Soon shall the night be gone,
   And we with Jesus reign;
The marriage supper of the Lamb
   Shall banish ev'ry pain.

———

BAPTISM.

49.—8, 7.

1 JESUS, hail! exalted Saviour,
   We adore Thy matchless grace;
Thou didst bear our misbehaviour,
   Suff'ring in our room and place;
      Wrath and terror
   Sunk Thy soul in deep disgrace.

2 For us Thou didst bear the horrors
   Of the judgment unto blood;
Who can understand the sorrows
   Of Thy soul in wrath's deep flood?
      Fearful anguish!
   Only fully known to God.

3 Yet, through grace, we know in measure,
   What Thy love for us hath done,

And we hope, through Thy good pleasure,
To behold Thee on Thy throne,
And for ever,
Sing the vict'ries Thou hast won.

4 By Thy Spirit's operation,
Into death, Thy death, baptiz'd,
Risen with Thee, Thy Salvation
Is by us no more despis'd:
Therefore baptism
Must by us be dearly priz'd.

50.—7s.

1 PRECIOUS Jesus! here we are,
Come to witness and declare
We are Thine, redeem'd with blood,
Call'd and prov'd the sons of God.

2 Wrath and vengeance on Thee fell,
That we might be sav'd from hell:
And shall we disdain to own
What Thou hast to us made known?

3 Jesus, ere He gave His blood,
Was immers'd in Jordan's flood;
There, and in that way, to show
All He had to undergo.

4 In the watery grave we see,
Looking through it, Lord, to Thee,
Jesus, overwhelm'd in blood,
Sunk in wrath's tremendous flood.

5 Thanks, eternal thanks to Thee,
That we thus can plainly see

Mercy, truth, and justice meet,
All to make Thy bride complete.

51.—6, 6, 8, 6.

1 As sinners sav'd by grace,
   And made alive to God,
Thy righteousness we would embrace,
   And tread the heav'nly road.

2 Thy wisdom did ordain
   This solemn rite to show
How Thou wast plung'd in wrath and pain,
   To save our souls from woe.

3 We come Thy name to own,
   And solemnly confess,
Thou art our Life, our joy, our Crown,
   Our Strength and Righteousness.

52.—6, 6, 8, 6.

1 One baptism we own,
   A sacred, solemn sign
Of what the Saviour 's undergone,
   To wash away our sin.

2 His overwhelming pain,
   And burial we see;
His rising from the grave again,
   To set His members free.

3 He hid our guilt from view,
   And buried all our sin;

And He ordained this way to show
That we are one with Him.

4 Then here by faith we view,
That Christians all are dead
To Satan, sin, and Moses too,
Through Christ their living Head.

5 And rising from the flood
Doth solemnly maintain
Their life is hid with Christ in God,
And they shall with Him reign.

53.—7s.

1 For us Jesus was baptiz'd
For us He was agoniz'd;
Mighty vengeance, like a flood,
Overwhelm'd the Lamb of God.

2 Come, ye saints, with wonder view
What the Lord has done for you;
View the mighty waters roll,
Breaking in upon His soul.

3 View the swelling floods of wrath
Sinking Jesus into death;
Grief Him cover'd like a grave,
When He died your souls to save.

4 This was baptism indeed;
Well might mountains shake with dread;
Baptism serves in type to show,
What our Lord did undergo.

2 From Thy word with food provided,
  May we feed thereon, and grow;
And by Thee, the Saviour, guided,
  Through the pathless desert go:
    While the gospel
  Charms our heart from all below.

3 Saviour, keep all evil from us,
  Go before us in the way,
'Till we reach the land of promise,
  Be Thy word our guide and stay;
    Joy and triumph
  Shall be our's in that blest day.

4 Then Thy people's griefs are over,
  Then Thy people cease to fight;
In that day Thou wilt discover
  All Thy glory to our sight—
    God our portion,
  God our everlasting light !

58.—6, 6, 6, 6, 8, 8.

On what has now been sown,
  Thy blessing, Lord, bestow;
The power is Thine alone,
  To make it spring and grow;
Do Thou the gracious harvest raise,
And Thou alone shalt have the praise !

59.—8, 6.

1 Blest be the dear uniting love
  That will not let us part:
Our bodies may far off remove;
  We still are one in heart.

2 Join'd in one Spirit to our Head
   We wait His truth to know,
That we may in His footsteps tread,
   And do His work below.

3 O, let us ever walk with Him,
   And nothing know beside;
Nothing desire, nothing esteem,
   But Jesus crucify'd.

4 Then let us hasten to the day,
   Which shall our Lord restore
When death and sin shall pass away,
   And we shall part no more.

60.—8s.

1 LORD, now we part in Thy blest name,
In which we here together came;
Grant us our few remaining days,
To work Thy will, and spread Thy praise.

2 Teach us, in life and death, to bless
The Lord our Strength and Righteousness,
And grant us all to meet above,
Where we shall ever sing Thy love!

61.—6, 6, 8, 6.

1 ONCE more, before we part,
   We'll bless the Saviour's name;
Record His mercies, ev'ry heart;
   Sing, ev'ry tongue, the same.

2 Hoard up His sacred word,
   And feed thereon, and grow;

Go on still more to know the Lord,
And practise what we know.

62.—7s.

1 CHRISTIAN brethren, ere we part,
Ev'ry voice, and ev'ry heart
One glad hymn to God should raise,
One high note of grateful praise.

2 Here we all may meet no more;
But there is a happier shore,
Where, releas'd from toil and pain,
Brethren, we shall meet again.

3 By the Spirit Who has won
Us to God thro' Christ the Son,
Glad we raise the song again,
Hallelujah! and amen!

63.—8, 7, 8, 7, 7, 7.

SAVIOUR, follow with Thy blessing
Truth deliver'd in Thy name;
Thus the word, Thy pow'r possessing,
Shall declare from whence it came:
Mighty let the Gospel be,
All subduing, Lord, to Thee!

64.—8, 7.

1 LORD, dismiss us with Thy blessing;
Fill our hearts with joy and peace;
Let us each, Thy love possessing,
Triumph in redeeming grace!
O refresh us,
Trav'lling through this wilderness.

2 Thanks we give, and adoration,
  For the Gospel's joyful sound.
May the fruits of Thy salvation
  In our hearts and lives abound!
    Ever faithful
    To the truth may we be found!

3 So, whene'er the signal's given.
  Us from earth to call away,
Borne aloft by grace to heaven,
  Glad the summons to obey,
    We shall ever
    Reign with Thee in endless day!

65.—8, 7.

1 MAY the grace of Christ our Saviour,
  And the Father's boundless love,
With the Holy Spirit's favour,
  Rest upon us from above!

2 Thus may we abide in union
  With each other and the Lord,
And possess, in sweet communion,
  Joys which earth can ne'er afford.

66.—8, 7.

1 WHILE to sev'ral paths dividing,
  We our pilgrimage pursue,
May our Shepherd, safely guiding,
  Keep His scatter'd flock in view!
May the bond of blest communion
  Ev'ry distant soul embrace,
'Till in everlasting union,
  We attain our resting-place.

2 O 'tis sweet, each other aiding,
    In companionship to move,
One desire each heart pervading,
    One, our Lord, our faith, our love:
Sweet when each can bend, imploring
    Soothing for his brother's pain,
And, the stumbling soul restoring,
    Cheer him to the race again.

67.—8s.

1 Dismiss us with Thy blessing, Lord;
  Help us to feed upon Thy word;
  All that has been amiss forgive,
  And let Thy truth within us live!

2 Though we are guilty, Thou art good;
  Wash all our works in Jesu's blood;
  Give ev'ry fetter'd soul release,
  And bid us all, "Depart in peace!"

68.—8s.

Blessings for ever on the Lamb,
Who bore the curse for wretched man;
While angels sing His sacred name,
May ev'ry creature say, Amen!

69.—8, 7, 7, 4.

Of Thy love some gracious token
    Grant us, Lord, before we go;
Bless Thy word which has been spoken,
    Life and peace on all bestow.
When we join the world again,
May our hearts with Thee remain:

O direct us,
And protect us,
Till we gain the heav'nly shore,
Where Thy people want no more.

70.—6, 6, 6, 6, 8, 8.

1 To Thee our wants are known,
  From Thee are all our powers,
Accept what is Thine own,
  And pardon what is ours;
Our praises, Lord, and prayers receive,
And to Thy word Thy blessing give.

2 O grant that each of us,
  · Now met before Thee here,
May meet together thus,
  When Thou and Thine appear;
And follow Thee to heav'n our home,
E'en so, Amen, Lord Jesus, come.

71.—8s.

1 WE bless Thee, Lord, that we have met
Once more before Thy mercy-seat,
Thy ransom'd family, to raise
In Jesu's name our song of praise.

2 And now Thy blessing we implore,
To guard and keep us evermore;
Into Thine hand our souls commend,
To guide, and strengthen, and defend.

3 Through all the dangers of the night
Through the temptations of the light,

Through every snare, from every ill,
Thou, Lord, shalt be our Saviour still.

4 Once more, for all Thy love hath done,
Thy mercies past, or yet unknown;
For all Thy goodness, gracious Lord,
For ever be Thy name ador'd!

72.—8s.

GREAT Father of mercies, we bow
With thanks for our headship above;
Nor less, Holy Jesus, art Thou
The object of praise and of love!
In the three glorious persons in God,
(Whose sov'reignty all shall adore);
Through Christ, and by faith in His blood,
We'll glory and boast evermore.

73.—8, 8, 6.

HENCEFORWARD, till the Lord shall come
To take His whole redeemed home,
(With Him, for ever then);
The Lord send blessings from above,
The Father's, Son's, and Spirit's love,
Be with us all. Amen.

FOR TRIAL. IN SOLITUDE.

8, 6.

1 JESUS, my sorrow lies too deep
    For human ministry ;
It knows not how to tell itself
    To any but to Thee.

2 Thou dost remember still, amid
    The glories of God's throne,
The sorrows of mortality,
    For they were once Thine own.

3 Yes, for as if Thou would'st be God,
    E'en in Thy misery,
There's been no sorrow but Thine own
    Untouch'd by sympathy.

4 Jesus, my fainting spirit brings
    It's fearfulness to Thee,
Thine eye at least can penetrate
    The clouded mystery.   .

5 And is it not enough, enough,
    This holy sympathy ?
There is no sorrow e'er so deep
    But I may bring to Thee.

SECOND PART.—ASSENT.

1 IT is enough—my precious Lord,
    Thy tender sympathy— .
My ev'ry sin and sorrow can
    Devolve itself on Thee.

2 As God, Thou graspedst e'en the whole
    Of human misery,
Thine own alone lay desolate,
    That Thou mightst pitied be.

3 Thy risen life but whets Thee more
   For kindly sympathy,
Thy love unhinder'd rests upon
   Each *bruised* "Branch in Thee."

4 Jesus, Thou hast avail'd to probe
   My deepest malady,
It freely flows, more freely finds
   Thy gracious remedy.

————

PRAYER.

1 LORD ! let my heart still turn to Thee,
   In all my hours of waking thought !
Nor let this heart e'er wish to flee,
   To think, or feel, where thou art not !

2 In every hour of pain or woe,
   When nought on earth this heart can cheer,
When sighs will burst, and tears will flow,
   Lord, hush the sigh, and chase the tear !

3 In every dream of earthly bliss,
   Do Thou, dear Saviour, present be !
Nor let me dream of happiness
   On earth. without the thought of Thee !

4 To my last lingering thought at night,
   Do Thou, Lord Jesus, still be near,
And ere the dawn of opening light,
   In still small accents wake mine ear !

5 Whene'er I read Thy sacred word,
   Bright on the page in glory shine !
And let me say, " *This precious Lord
In all His full salvation 's mine.*"

6 And when before the throne I kneel,
   Hear from that throne of grace my prayer ;
And let each hope of heaven I feel,
   Burn with the thought to meet Thee there.

7 Thus teach me, Lord, to look to Thee,
   In ev'ry hour of waking thought,
Nor let me ever wish to be,
   To think or feel where Thou art not ! AMEN.

APPENDIX.

1.—8s.

1 O GRACE Divine ! the Saviour shed
   His life-blood on the cursed tree ;
Bow'd on the cross His blessed head,
   And died, to make His brethren free.

2 Through suffering there beneath His feet,
   He trod the fierce avenger down:
There power itself and weakness meet,
   Emblem of each, yon thorny crown.

3 Fruit of the curse, the tangled thorn,
   Shew'd that He bore its deadly sting ;
The crown, 'mid Israel's cruel scorn,
   Mark'd Him as earth's anointed King.

4 O blessed hour ! when all the earth,
   Its rightful Heir shall yet receive ;
When every tongue shall own His worth,
   And all creation cease to grieve.

5 Thou, dearest Saviour ! Thou alone
   Can'st give Thy weary people rest ;
And, Lord, till Thou art on the throne,
   This groaning earth can ne'er be blest.

A

2.—8, 7.

1 'Twas the Holy Ghost who taught us
  How the vail is rent in twain
By the Lord whose blood hath bought us,
  Him who died and rose again,
And at Thy right hand, O God,
Pleads for us His precious blood.

2 Through the Saviour's blood appearing
  Ever on the Mercy-seat,
We approach Thee, nothing fearing,
  For we know His work complete:
Father! in Thy love we rest,
In Thy Son's redemption blest.

3.—8, 6.

1 What grace, O Lord, and beauty shone
  Around Thy steps below,
What patient love was seen in all
  Thy life and death of woe.

2 For ever on Thy burden'd heart
  A weight of sorrow hung,
Yet no ungentle murm'ring word
  Escaped Thy silent tongue.

3 Thy foes might hate, despise, revile,
  Thy friends unfaithful prove,
Unwearied in forgiveness still,
  Thy heart could only love.

4 O give us hearts to love like Thee,
  Like Thee, O Lord, to grieve
Far more for others' sins, than all
  The wrongs that we receive.

5 One with Thyself, may every eye
    In us, thy brethren, see
That gentleness and grace that springs
    From union, Lord, with Thee.

4.—8, 6.

1 Sweet was the hour, O Lord, to Thee,
    At Sychar's lonely well,
When a poor outcast heard Thee there
    Thy great salvation tell.

2 Thither she came; but O, her heart,
    All fill'd with earthly care,
Dream'd not of Thee, nor thought to find
    The Hope of Israel there.

3 Lord! 'twas Thy power unseen that drew
    The stray one to that place,
In solitude to learn from Thee
    The secrets of Thy grace.

4 There Jacob's erring daughter found
    Those streams unknown before,
The waterbrooks of life that make
    The weary thirst no more.

5 And, Lord, to us, as vile as she,
    Thy gracious lips have told
That mystery of love, reveal'd
    At Jacob's well of old.

6 In spirit, Lord, we 've sat with Thee
    Beside the springing well
Of life and peace—and heard Thee there
    Its healing virtues tell.

7 Dead to the world, we dream no more
  Of earthly pleasures now ;
Our deep, divine, unfailing spring
  Of grace and glory, Thou !

8 No hope of rest in aught beside,
  No beauty, Lord, we see,
And like Samaria's daughter seek,
  And find our all in Thee.

5.—8, 8, 6.

1 CHILDREN of light, arise and shine !
Your birth, your hopes, are all divine,
  Your home is in the skies.
O then, for heavenly glory born,
Look down on all with holy scorn
  That earthly spirits prize.

2 With Christ, with glory full in view,
O what is all the world to you?
  What is it all but loss?
Come on, then, cleave no more to earth,
Nor wrong your high celestial birth,
  Ye pilgrims of the cross.

3 The cross is ours; we bear it now:
But did not He beneath it bow,
  And suffer there at last?
All that we feel can Jesus tell ;
His gracious soul remembers well
  The sorrows of the past.

4 O blessed Lord, we yet shall reign,
Redeem'd from sorrow, sin, and pain,
  And walk with Thee in white.

We suffer now, but O at last
We 'll bless Thee, Lord, for all the past,
   And own our cross was light.

6.—8s.

1 THOU vain deceitful world, farewell !
   Thine idle joys no more we love:
By faith in brighter worlds we dwell,
   In spirit find our home above.

2 Jesus, we go with Thee to taste
   Of joy supreme that never dies ;
Our feet still press the weary waste,
   Our heart, our home, are in the skies.

3 And O while on to Zion's hill
   The toilsome path of life we tread,
Around us, loving Father, still,
   Thy circling wings of mercy spread.

4 From day to day, from hour to hour,
   O may our rising spirits prove
The strength of Thine almighty power,
   The sweetness of Thy saving love !

7.—8s.

1 'TIS night—but O the joyful morn
   Will soon our waiting spirits cheer ;
Yon gleams of coming glory warn
   Thy saints, O Lord, that Thou art near.

2 Lord of our hearts, beloved of Thee,
   Weary of earth, we sigh to rest,
Supremely happy, safe and free,
   For ever on Thy tender breast:

3 To see Thee, love Thee, feel Thee, near,
    Nor dread, as now, Thy transient stay,
To dwell beyond the reach of fear,
    Lest joy should wane, or pass away.

4 Children of hope, beloved Lord!
    In Thee we live, we glory now,
Our joy, our rest, our great reward,
    Our diadem of beauty Thou!

5 And when exalted, Lord, with thee,
    Thy royal throne at last we share,
To everlasting Thou shalt be
    Our diadem, our glory, there.

. 8.—8s.

1 O GOD, whose wondrous name is LOVE,
    Whose hands have fashion'd us anew,
Before Thy face now stands the Lamb,
    Whom sinful man once pierced and slew:
Thy own dear Son Thou didst not spare,
How shalt Thou cease for us to care?

2 Our Heavenly Father, grant us all
    The new-born babe's simplicity!
The doubtful mind be far from us,
    Who boast a God that cannot lie!
Array'd in comeliness divine,
On Jesus' bosom we recline.

3 Thou art the potter, we the clay,
    Thy will be our's, Thy truth our light,
Thy love the fountain of our joy,
    Thine arm a safe-guard day and night,
Till Thou shalt wipe our tears away,
And Jesus bring eternal day.

9.—11s.

1 THE night is far spent, and the day is at hand :
   Already the dawn may be seen in the sky ;
Rejoice then, ye saints, 'tis your Lord's own command ;
   Rejoice, for the coming of Jesus draws nigh.

2 What a day will that be when the Saviour appears !
   How welcome to those who have shared in His cross !
A crown incorruptible then will be theirs,
   A rich compensation for suffering and loss.

3 What is loss in this world, when compared to that day,
   To the glory that then will from heaven be reveal'd ?
" The Saviour is coming," His people may say ;
   " The Lord whom we look for, our Sun and our
      Shield."

4 O pardon us, Lord ! that our love to Thy name
   Is so faint, with *so much* our affections to move !
Our deadness should fill us with grief and with shame,
   So much to be loved, *and so little to love.*

5 O kindle within us a holy desire,
   Like that which was found in Thy people of old,
Who felt all Thy love, and whose hearts were on fire,
   While they waited impatient Thy face to behold.

10.—8s.

1 DEAR Lord, amid the throng that press'd
   Around Thee on the cursed tree,
Some loyal, loving hearts were there,
   Some pitying eyes that wept for Thee.

2 Like them may we rejoice to own
   Our dying Lord, though crown'd with thorn,
Like Thee, Thy blessed self, endure
   The cross with all its joy or scorn.

3 Thy cross, Thy lonely path below,
    Shew what Thy brethren all should be,
  Pilgrims on earth, disown'd by those
    Who see no beauty, Lord, in Thee,

11.—8, 6.

1 SAVIOUR, I long to follow Thee,
    Daily Thy cross to bear,
  And count all else, whate'er it be,
    Unworthy of my care.

2 I am not now my own, but *Thine*,
    The purchase of Thy blood,
  And made by grace and love divine
    A son and heir of God.

3 Thy Spirit, too, the present seal
    Of all the Father's love,
  Dwells in my soul, and does reveal
    The glorious rest above.

4 My sins lie buried in the grave,
    From condemnation free,
  Life, strength, and grace, I in Thee have,
    For I am *one* with Thee.

5 O teach me so the power to know,
    Of risen life with Thee,
  Not I may live, while here below,
    But Christ may live in me.

12.—8s.

1 O WONDROUS hour ! when, Jesus, Thou,
    Co-equal with th' eternal God,
  Beneath our sin vouchsafed to bow,
    And in our nature bore the rod.

2 On Thee, the Father's blessed Son,
    Jehovah's utmost anger fell:
That all was borne, that all is done,
    Thine agony, Thy cross can tell.

3 Thy cross! Thy cross! 'tis there we see
    What Thou, beloved Saviour! art:
There all the love that dwells in Thee,
    Was labouring in Thy breaking heart.

4 For us it strove—our life we owe,
    Our joy, our glory, all to Thee:
Thy sufferings in that hour of woe,
    Thy victory, Lord, have made us free.

13.—8, 6.

1 FAREWELL, ye fleeting joys of earth,
    We 've seen the Saviour's face,
Beheld Him with the eye of faith,
    And know His love and grace.

2 Forth from His Father's loving breast,
    To bear our sin and shame,
To face a cold unfeeling world,
    The heavenly Stranger came.

3 This earth to Him, the Lord of all,
    No kindly welcome gave ;
In Judah's land the Saviour found
    No shelter but the grave.

4 Then fare thee well, thou faithless world!
    Thine evil eye could see
No grace in Him whose dying love
    Hath wean'd our hearts from thee.

5 The cross was His ; and O 'tis ours
   Its weight on earth to bear,
And glory in the thought that He
   Was once a sufferer there.

14.—10, 10, 11, 11.

1 In weakness and trial,
   With God we may plead ;
No fear of denial,
   We 're sure to succeed:
For though we oft grieve Him,
   His promise is clear,
And love will believe Him:
   Our Father will hear.

2 'Gainst the giant-like might
   Of our foes, we can bring,
As our weapons of fight,
   A stone and a sling.
Should this have dismay'd us,
   Our souls it may cheer,
That, call'd on to aid us,
   Our Father will hear.

3 Our calls may be weak
   As the voice of a child :
And all that we speak
   Must by sin be defiled.
Yet Christ for us pleading,
   We may persevere,
Through Him interceding,
   Our Father will hear.

15.—8s.

1 WELL may we count the world but loss,
  And gladly join His praise to sing,
But for our sins endured the cross,
  And dying took from death its sting.

2 Pleading that cross, the soul may dare
  Appeal to covenanted love ;
For He who bore our burden there
  Now lives to intercede above.

3 Strong in that cross, the soul may dare
  Sin's dark device, and Satan's might,
Can see unmoved the opening grave,
  And call earth's worst affliction light.

4 Wise in that cross, the soul may trace
  Th' unfolded plan of power and love ;
And see in our *Emmanuel's* face,
  The glory angels see above.

16.—8, 6.

1 HOPELESS and outcast once we lay,
  Worthy Thy hate and scorn,
But love like Thine could find a way
  To rescue and adorn.

2 Dear Saviour, from Thy bleeding veins
  A living fountain flows,
To wash Thy Bride from all her stains,
  And soothe her deepest woes.

3 Cleansed from her sins, renew'd by grace,
  Thy royal throne above,

Dear Saviour, is her destin'd place,
Her sweet abode Thy love.

4 Thine eye, in that unclouded day,
Shall, with supreme delight,
Thy fair and glorious Bride survey,
Unblemish'd in Thy sight.

17.—8, 4, 8, 4, 8, 8, 8, 4.

1 ONE there is above all others—
O how He loves!
His is love beyond a brother's—
O how He loves!
Earthly friends may fail or leave us,
One day soothe, the next day grieve us,
But this Friend will ne'er deceive us—
O how He loves!

2 'Tis eternal life to know Him—
O how He loves!
Think, O think how much we owe Him—
O how He loves!
With His precious blood he bought us,
In the wilderness He sought us,
To His fold he safely brought us—
O how He loves!

3 We have found a friend in Jesus—
O how He loves!
'Tis His great delight to bless us—
O how He loves!
How our hearts delight to hear Him
Bid us dwell in safety near Him;
Why should we distrust or fear Him?—
O how He loves!

4 Through His name we are forgiven—
  O how He loves!
Backward shall our foes be driven—
  O how He loves!
Best of blessings he 'll provide us,
Nought but good shall e'er betide us—
Safe to glory He will guide us—
  O HOW HE LOVES!

18.—8s.

1 FROM every stormy wind that blows,
  From every swelling tide of woes,
  There is a calm, a sweet retreat;
  'Tis found beneath the Mercy-seat.

2 There is a place where Jesus sheds
  The oil of gladness on our heads,
  A place than all besides more sweet—
  It is the blood-stain'd Mercy-seat.

3 There is a spot where spirits blend,
  And friend holds fellowship with friend;
  Though sunder'd far, by faith they meet
  Around our common Mercy-seat.

4 Ah! whither could we flee for aid
  When tempted, desolate, dismay'd?
  Or how the host of hell defeat,
  Had suffering saints no Mercy-seat?

5 There, there, on eagles' wings we soar,
  And time and sense seem all no more,
  And heaven comes down our souls to greet,
  And glory crowns the Mercy-seat.

19.—6, 6, 8, 6.

1 WHAT rais'd the wondrous thought,
    Or who did it suggest?
  "That we, the church, to glory brought,
    Should WITH the Son be blest."

2 O God! the thought was Thine!
    Thine only it could be:
  Fruit of the wisdom, love Divine,
    Peculiar unto Thee:

3 For sure, no other mind,
    For thoughts so bold, so free,
  Greatness or strength could ever find,
    Thine, therefore, it must be.

4 The motives too Thine own!
    The plan, the counsel, Thine!—
  "Made for Thy Son, bone of His bone,"
    In glory bright to shine.

5 Jesus! with great delight
    Thy bride preparing, see,
  Upon Thy throne, in glory bright,
    Thy bosom friend to be.

6 Father, we sing Thy love,
    Seal'd with the Holy Ghost;
  Nor fear (Thy choice He will approve)
    The Bridegroom's love to boast.

20.—8. 7.

"Behold the Lamb of God."

1 LAMB of God! our souls adore Thee
    While upon Thy face we gaze;
  There the Father's love and glory
    Shine in all their brightest rays;

Thy almighty power and wisdom
  All creation's works proclaim;
Heaven and earth alike confess Thee
  As the ever great "I AM."

2 Lamb of God! thy Father's bosom
  Ever was Thy dwelling place;
His delight, in Him rejoicing,
  One with Him in power and grace:
O what wondrous love and mercy!
  Thou didst lay Thy glory by,
And for us didst come from heaven,
  As the Lamb of God to die.

3 Lamb of God! when we behold Thee
  Lowly in the manger laid,
Wand'ring, as a homeless stranger,
  In the world Thy hands had made;
When we see Thee in the garden
  In thine agony of blood,
At thy grace we are confounded,
  Holy, spotless, Lamb of God.

4 When we see Thee, as the victim,
  Bound to the accursed tree,
For our guilt and folly stricken,
  All our judgment borne by Thee,
Lord, we learn, with hearts adoring,
  All Thy love in drops of blood;
Glory, glory everlasting,
  Be to Thee, thou Lamb of God!

SECOND PART.

"I saw a Lamb as it had been slain." Rev. v. 6.

1 LAMB of God! Thou now art seated
  High upon Thy Father's throne;

All Thy gracious work completed,
  All Thy mighty vict'ry won:
Every knee in heaven is bending
  To the Lamb for sinners slain ;
Every voice and harp is swelling
  " Worthy is the Lamb to reign !"

2 Lord, in all Thy power and glory,
    Still Thy thoughts and eyes are here ;
  Watching o'er Thy ransom'd people,
    To Thy gracious heart so dear:
  Thou for us art interceding,
    Everlasting is Thy love ;
  And a blessed rest preparing,
    In our Father's house above.

3 Lamb of God ; Thou soon in glory
    Wilt to this sad earth return ;
  All Thy foes shall quake before Thee,
    All that now despise Thee mourn:
  Then Thy saints shall rise to meet Thee,
    With Thee in Thy kingdom reign ;
  Thine the praise, and Thine the glory,
    Lamb of God for sinners slain.

21.—8s.

" For yet a little while." Heb. x. 37.

1 "A LITTLE while," our Lord shall come,
    And we shall wander here no more ;
  He 'll take us to our Father's home,
    Where He for us has gone before—
  To dwell with Him, to see His face,
  And sing the glories of His grace.

2 " A little while "—he 'll come again:
    Let us the precious hours redeem ;

Our only grief to give Him pain,
  Our joy to serve and follow Him.
Watching and ready may we be,
As those that long their Lord to see.

3 " A little while "—'t will soon be past,
  Why should we shun the promised cross?
O let us in His footsteps haste,
  Counting for Him all else but loss:
O how will recompense His smile,
The sufferings of this "little while."

4 " A little while "—come, Saviour, come!
  For Thee Thy Bride has tarried long;
Take Thy poor wearied pilgrims home,
  To sing the new eternal song,
To see Thy glory, and to be
In every thing conform'd to Thee!

22.—8, 6.

1 O WHAT a lonely path were ours,
  Could we, O Father, see
No home of rest beyond it all,
  No guide or help in Thee!

2 But Thou art near, and with us still,
  To keep us on the way
That leads along this vale of tears,
  To the bright world of day.

3 There shall Thy glory, O our God!
  Break fully on our view;
And we, Thy saints, rejoice to find
  That all Thy word was true.

4 There Jesus, on His heavenly throne,
  Our wond'ring eyes shall see:

b

While we the blest associates there,
　Of all His joy shall be.

5 Sweet hope! we leave without a sigh
　A blighted world like this;
To bear the cross, despise the shame,
　For all that weight of bliss.

6 Yet little do Thy saints at best,
　Endure, O Lord, for Thee;
Whose suffering soul bore all our sins
　And sorrows on the tree;

7 Who faced our fierce, our ruthless foe,
　Unaided, and alone;
To win us for Thy crown of joy,
　To raise us to Thy throne.

23.—8s.

1 'Tis finish'd all—our souls to win
　His life the blessed Jesus gave;
Then, rising, left His people's sin
　Behind Him in His opening grave.

2 Past suffering now, the tender heart
　Of Jesus on His Father's throne,
Still in *our* sorrow bears a part,
　And feels it as He felt His own.

3 Sweet thought! we have a Friend above,
　Our weary falt'ring steps to guide;
Who follows with the eye of love
　The little flock for whom He died.

4 O, Jesus, teach us more and more
　On Thee alone to cast our care;
And gazing on Thy cross, adore
　The wondrous grace that brought Thee there.

24.—8s.

1 O WHAT a thrill of deep delight,
    Through the bright hosts of glory ran,
When Jesus, in the fearful fight,
    Had finish'd all for ransom'd man!

2 "'Tis FINISH'D! FINISH'D!" sweetly rung
    Through the whole world of bliss above;
And seraphim broke forth and sung
    The glories of redeeming love.

3 Thus heaven rejoiced; while yet below,
    Jesus, Thy saints in deep dismay
Beheld the scene of mighty woe,
    'Till faith, and all but love, gave way.

4 Yes; it was love alone that led
    Thy brethren, Lord, to seek Thy grave;
But every gleam of hope had fled,
    For Thou, they deem'd, had'st fail'd to save.

5 'Twas Thine own arm of power that broke,
    Lord, ere they came, the grave's control;
'Twas Thine own blessed voice that spoke,
    "PEACE, PEACE!" to each reviving soul.

6 Peace was their portion, peace is ours,
    We, like Thine earlier brethren, see
Our victory won o'er Satan's powers,
    Our blessedness secured by Thee.

7 In the pure blood on Calv'ry shed,
    Wash'd from our sin, beloved Lord;
We, with Thyself, our living Head,
    Wait for our glorious bright reward.

25.—8, 6.

1 " THE LORD IS RISEN "—O what joy
   These blessed tidings give !
He died our en'mies to destroy,
   He lives, we therefore live.

2 " THE LORD IS RISEN "—death and sin
   And hell all conquer'd are ;
He 's gone the holiest within,
   Our mansion to prepare.

3 " THE LORD IS RISEN "—see Him sit
   Upon the Father's throne:
All worship at His pierced feet,
   And Lord our Jesus own.

4 " THE LORD IS RISEN"—risen too
   With Him from sin and death,
Let us the heavenly things pursue,
   And die to all beneath.

5 Our place is with Him on the throne,
   There, with the Lord we love ;
As strangers here ourselves we own,
   Our hearts, our home, above.

26.—8, 6.

1 YE trembling saints who love the Lord,
   Chase all your fears away ;
For lo ! the tomb is vacant now—
   The place where Jesus lay.

2 Thus low the Lord of life was brought—
   Such wonders love can do—
There cold in death that bosom lay
   Which throbb'd and bled for you.

3 Then raise your eyes, and tune your songs,
   For Jesus lives again;
Not all the powers of death and hell
   The Conqueror could detain.

4 Exalted far above the skies,
   Behold your living Head—
The Lamb upon the Father's throne,
   Who dwelt among the dead.

27.—8, 7.

1 " ABBA, Father," we approach Thee
   In our Saviour's precious name,
We, Thy children, here assembling,
   Now Thy promised blessing claim.
From our sins His blood hath wash'd us,
   'Tis through Him our souls draw nigh;
And Thy Spirit too has taught us,
   " Abba Father" thus to cry.

2 Once as prodigals we wander'd
   In our folly far from Thee;
But Thy grace, o'er sin abounding,
   Rescued us from misery:
Thou Thy prodigals hast pardon'd,
   Kiss'd us with a Father's love;
Kill'd the fatted calf, and call'd us
   E'er to dwell with Thee above.

3 Clothed in garments of salvation,
   At Thy table is our place;
We rejoice, and Thou rejoicest,
   In the riches of Thy grace.
" It is meet," we hear Thee saying,
   " We should merry be and glad;
I have found my once lost children,
   Now they live who once were dead."

4 " Abba, Father !" all adore Thee,
    All rejoice in heaven above ;
While in us they learn the wonders
    Of Thy wisdom, grace, and love.
Soon before Thy throne assembled,
    All Thy children shall proclaim ;
" Glory, everlasting glory,
    Be to God and to the Lamb !"

28.—8, 6.

1 THY sympathies and hopes are ours ;
    Dear Lord ! we wait to see
Creation, all—below, above,
    Redeem'd and blest by Thee.

2 Our longing eyes would fain behold
    That bright and blessed brow,
Once wrung with bitterest anguish, wear
    Its crown of glory now.

3 Why linger then ? come, Saviour, come,
    Responsive to our call ;
Come, claim Thine ancient power, and reign,
    The Heir and Lord of all.

29.—6, 6, 6, 6, 8, 8.

1   Joy to the ransom'd earth !
        Messiah fills the throne ;
    His all excelling worth,
        Ye joyful nations, own.
    Ye sons of men, break forth and sing
    The praises of your God and king !

2   Behold ! the desert smiles
      To hear His welcome voice,
    And all the list'ning isles
      Beneath His love rejoice.
Ye dwellers in the islands, sing
The glories of your heavenly King !

3   To gain a royal crown
      Of glory for His Bride,
    The foe He trampled down,
      And conquer'd when He died.
O earth, rejoice ! break forth and sing
The conquests of your dying King !

4   Rejoice beneath the eye
      Of Jesus and His Bride,
    His Queen, enthron'd on high,
      In glory at His side !
Blest in His love, ye nations, sing
Hosanna to your glorious King !

30.—8, 6.

1 Through Israel's land, the Lord of all
     A homeless wanderer past,
  Then closed His life of sorrow here,
     On Calvary, at last.

2 O Zion ! when Thy Saviour came
     In grace and love to Thee,
  No beauty in Thy royal Lord
     Thy faithless eye could see.

3 Yet onward, in His path of grace,
     The holy Sufferer went,
  To feel, at last, that love on Thee
     Had all in vain been spent.

4 Yet not in vain—o'er Israel's land
  The glory yet will shine ;
And He, thy once rejected King,
  Messiah shall be thine.

5 His chosen Bride, ordain'd with Him
  To reign o'er all the earth,
Shall first be framed, ere thou shalt know,
  Thy Saviour's matchless worth.

6 Then thou, beneath the peaceful reign
  Of Jesus and His Bride,
Shalt sound His grace and glory forth,
  To all the earth beside.

7 The nations to thy glorious light,
  O Zion, yet shall throng,
And all the list'ning islands wait
  To catch the joyful song.

8 The name of Jesus yet shall ring
  Through earth and heaven above ;
And all His ransom'd people know
  The sabbath of His love.

31.—8, 6.

1 CHILDREN of light, awake ! awake !
  Ye slumbering virgins, rise ;
Go, meet the royal Bridegroom now,
  And shew that ye are wise.

2 Like foolish virgins, ye have fail'd
  Your holy watch to keep ;
And lo, He comes, and almost finds
  Your languid souls asleep !

3 Through love, the Man of Sorrows oft
　Hath watch'd and wept for you ;
Then gave away His life, to prove
　That all that love was true.

4 Then wake ! for lo, the midnight cry
　Of warning in the air
Bids all His church to greet Him now,
　Their dying lamps prepare !

32.—7s

1 HARK ! the song of Jubilee,
　Loud as mighty thunders roar,
Or the fulness of the sea
　When it breaks upon the shore !
Hallelujah ! for the Lord
　God omnipotent shall reign:
Hallelujah ! let the word
　Echo round the earth and main !

2 Hallelujah !—hark ! the sound
　From the depth unto the skies,
Wakes above, beneath, around,
　All creation's harmonies !
See, Jehovah's banners furl'd,
　Sheath'd his sword: he speaks—'tis done ;
And the kingdoms of the world
　Are the kingdoms of the Son !

3 He shall reign from pole to pole
　With illimitable sway;
He shall reign, when like a scroll
　Yonder heavens shall pass away:
Then the end ;—beneath His rod,
　Man's last enemy shall fall ;
Hallelujah ! Christ in God,
　God in Christ is all in all.

33.—8, 6.

1 O EARTH, rejoice! from Salem see
   The chosen heralds bear
Glad tidings to the distant isles,
   That Salem's King is there.

2 Lo, Jacob's star, in vision seen
   By Balaam's wond'ring eye!
It bursts upon the nations now,
   The day-spring from on high.

3 A crown, but not a crown of thorn,
   Surrounds the Victor's brow;
That hand that once was pierced for sin,
   It wields the sceptre now.

4 But brighter honours far than those
   Of David's royal Son,
As Head of His anointed Bride,
   The Lord of Life hath won.

5 Though grace may shine in all His ways,
   With Israel's chosen race;
'Tis in His church alone we see,
   The full display of grace.

6 'Twas grace divine that made Him love,
   And choose her for His own;
Grace raised her from her low estate,
   And placed her on the throne.

34.—7, 7, 4, 4, bis.

Revelations xix.14.

1 Lo 'tis the heavenly army,
   The Lord of hosts attending,

'Tis He—the Lamb,
The great I AM,
With all His saints descending.
(*Lo 'tis the heavenly army!*)
To you, ye kings and nations,
Ye foes of Christ, assembling;
  The hosts of light,
  Prepared for fight,
Come with the cup of trembling.

ISRAEL.

2 Joy to His ancient people!
Your bonds He comes to sever—
  And now, 'tis done!
  The Lord hath won,
And ye are free for ever—
  (*Joy to his ancient people!*)

THE GENTILES.

Joy to the ransom'd nations!
The foe, the rav'ning lion,
  Is bound in chains
  While Jesus reigns,
King of the earth, in Zion.

THE CHURCH.

3 Joy to the church triumphant,
The Saviour's throne surrounding!
  They see his face,
  Adore his grace,
O'er all their sin abounding—
(*Joy to the church triumphant!*)
Crown'd with the mighty victor,
His royal glory sharing;

Each fills a throne,
His name alone
To heaven and earth declaring.

4 Praise to the Lamb for ever!
Bruised for our sin, and gory,
  Behold His brow,
  Encircled now
With all his crowns of glory—
(*Praise to the Lamb for ever!*)
Beneath His love reposing,
The whole redeem'd creation
  Is now at rest,
  For ever blest,
And sings His great salvation.

35.—7, 7, 4, 4, bis.

THE CHURCH.

1 BREAK forth, O earth, in praises!
Dwell on His wondrous story;
  The Saviour's name
  And love proclaim—
The King who reigns in glory—
(*Break forth, O earth in praises!*)
See on the throne beside Him,
O'er all her foes victorious,
  His royal Bride,
  For whom He died,
Like Him for ever glorious.

ISRAEL.

2 Ye of the seed of Jacob!
Behold the royal Lion
  Of Judah's line
  In glory shine,

And fill His throne in Zion.
(*Ye of the seed of Jacob!*)
Blest with Messiah's favour,
A ransom'd holy nation,
   . Your off'rings bring
    To Christ, your King,
The God of your salvation.

THE GENTILES.

3 Come, O ye kings! ye nations!
  With songs of gladness hail him,
    Ye Gentiles all,
    Before him fall,
  The royal Priest in Salem.
  (*Come, O ye kings! ye nations!*)
  O'er hell and death triumphant,
  Your conquering Lord hath risen;
    His praises sound,
    Whose power hath bound.
  Your ruthless foe in prison.

4 Hail to the King of Glory!
  Head of the new creation—
    Thy ways of grace
    We love to trace,
  And praise Thy great salvation.
  (*Hail to the King of Glory!*)
  Thy heart was press'd with sorrow,
  The bonds of death to sever,
    To make us free,
    That we might be
  Thy crown of joy for ever.

36.—8, 6.

1 'TIS He! the mighty Saviour comes,
  The victory now is won;

And lo, the throne of David waits
    For David's royal Son.

2 Thou blessed Heir of all the earth !
    Ascend Thine ancient throne,
And bid the willing nations now
    Thy peaceful sceptre own.

3 Shine forth in all Thy glory, Lord,
    That man at length may see
That joy, so long estranged from earth,
    Can only spring from Thee.

4 O happy day ! 'tis come at last,
    The reign of death is o'er ;
And sin that marr'd our sweetest joys
    Shall grieve our hearts no more.

5 Wash'd in Thy blood, the tribes of earth,
    With all the blest above,
Shall dwell in peace united now,
    One family of love.

6 Fruit of Thy toil, Thou bleeding Lamb !
    These joys we owe to Thee,
Then take the glory, Lord !—'tis Thine !—
    And shall for ever be.

37.—8s.

1 O WHAT a bright and blessed world
    This groaning earth of ours will be,
When from its throne the tempter hurl'd,
    Shall leave it all, O Lord, to Thee !

2 But brighter far that world above,
    Where we, as we are known, shall know ;
And, in the sweet embrace of love,
    Reign o'er this ransom'd earth below.

3 O blessed Lord ! with weeping eyes,
 That blissful hour we wait to see ;
While every worm or leaf that dies
 Tells of the curse, and calls for Thee.

4 Come, Saviour, then, o'er all below
 Shine brightly from Thy throne above ;
Bid heaven and earth Thy glory know
 And all creation feel Thy love.

38.—8, 6, 8, 6.
10, 6, 6, 6, 6, 7, 8.

1 O HASTE away, my brethren dear,
 And come to Canaan's shore ;
We 'll meet and sing for ever there,
 When all our toils are o'er.
O that will be joyful, joyful, joyful !
 O that will be joyful !
 To meet to part no more,
 To meet to part no more,
 On Canaan's happy shore.
And then sing Hallelujah,
With the friends that have gone before !

2 How sweet to hear the hallow'd theme
 That saints shall ever sing,
To hear their voices all proclaim
 Salvation to the King.
O that will be, &c.

3 Around His throne, all clothed in white,
 Will all His saints appear ;
And shining in his glory bright,
 Will see our Jesus there.
O that will be, &c.

4 Through heaven the shouts of angels ring,
 When sons to God are born ;

O what a company will sing
  On the millennial morn!
O that will be, &c.

5 In Canaan's happy land we'll meet,
  To chant this glorious lay;
Our hearts, well tuned, will sing so sweet,
  Through one eternal day.
O that will be, &c.

6 Through one eternal day we'll sing,
  And bless His sacred name,
With "Hallelujahs to the King!"
  And "Worthy is the Lamb!"
O that will be, &c.

39.—8, 6.

1 Sweeter, O Lord, than rest to Thee,
  While seated by the well,
Was Thine own task of love to all,
  Of grace and peace to tell.

2 One thoughtless heart that never knew
  The pulse of life before,
There learn'd to love—was taught to sigh
  For earthly joys no more.

3 Friend of the lost, O Lord, in Thee
  Samaria's daughter there
Found One whom love had drawn to earth,
  Her weight of guilt to bear.

4 Fair witness of Thy saving grace,
  In her, O Lord, we see,
The wandering soul by love subdued,
  The sinner drawn to Thee.

5 Through all that sweet and blessed scene,
 Dear Saviour, by the well,
More than enough the trembler finds,
 His guilty fears to quell.

6 There, in the full repose of faith,
 The soul delights to see,
Not only One who deeply loves,
 But *Love itself* in Thee.

7 Not One alone who feels for all,
 But fully knows the art
To meet the boundless sympathies
 Of every loving heart.

40.—8, 6.

1 'Tis past—the dark and dreary night,
 And, Lord, we hail Thee now,
Our Morning Star without a cloud
 Of sadness on Thy brow.

2 Thy path on earth, the cross, the grave,
 Thy sorrows all are o'er,
And, O sweet thought! Thine eye shall weep,
 Thy heart shall break no more.

3 Deep were those sorrows—deeper still
 The love that brought Thee low,
That bade the streams of life from Thee,
 A lifeless victim, flow.

4 The soldier, as he pierc'd Thee, proved
 Man's hatred, Lord, to Thee;
While in the blood that stain'd the spear
 Love, only love, we see.

5 Drawn from Thy pierc'd and bleeding side,
 That pure and cleansing flood

Speaks peace to every heart that knows
  The virtues of Thy blood.

6 Yet 'tis not that we know the joy
  Of cancell'd sin alone,
But, happier far, Thy saints are call'd
  To share Thy glorious throne.

7 So closely are we link'd in love,
  So wholly one with Thee,
That all *Thy* bliss, and glory then
  Our bright reward shall be.

8 Yes, when the storm of life is calm'd,
  The dreary desert pass'd,
Our way-worn hearts shall find in Thee
  Their full repose at last.

———

J. Wertheimer & Co., Printers, Finsbury Circus.

INDEX TO APPENDIX.